Praying
for Your
Children

BOOKS BY ELMER L. TOWNS

Knowing God Through Fasting

Praying the Scriptures Series

Praying Genesis

Praying Your Way Out of Bondage: Prayers from Exodus and Leviticus

Praying For a Second Chance: Prayers from Numbers and Deuteronomy

Praying With the Conquerors: Joshua, Judges, and Ruth

Praying the Book of Job

Praying the Psalms

*Praying the Proverbs, Song of Solomon,
and Ecclesiastes*

Praying the New Testament

Praying the Gospels

Praying the Book of Acts and the General Epistles

Praying Paul's Letters

Praying the Book of Revelation

Praying for Your Children

How to Build a Lasting Marriage: Lessons from Bible Couples

AVAILABLE FROM DESTINY IMAGE PUBLISHERS

Praying
for Your
Children

How To Pray Series

ELMER L. TOWNS
AND
DAVID EARLEY

DESTINY IMAGE® PUBLISHERS, INC.

P.O. Box 310, Shippensburg, PA 17257-0310

"Speaking to the Purposes of God for This Generation and for the Generations to Come."

This book and all other Destiny Image, Revival Press, MercyPlace, Fresh Bread, Destiny Image Fiction, and Treasure House books are available at Christian bookstores and distributors worldwide.

For a U.S. bookstore nearest you, call 1-800-722-6774.

For more information on foreign distributors, call 717-532-3040.

Or reach us on the Internet: www.destinyimage.com.

ISBN 10: 0-7684-3165-4
ISBN 13: 978-0-7684-3165-0

For Worldwide Distribution, Printed in the U.S.A.

1 2 3 4 5 6 7 8 9 10 11 / 13 12 11 10

Table of Contents

Victory Over Danger

How dangerous is it for children growing up in today's world? A lot more than when we parents were being raised. In school, children can get addicted to drugs; on the Internet, they may get addicted to pornography. And what about child abuse, AIDS, demonism, or even the influence of secularism? Will someone kill your child?

- A man killed 32 students and faculty at Virginia Tech before killing himself (2007).

- A man killed five children in an Amish one-room schoolhouse and critically injured five others (2006).

- Andrea Yates, a Houston, Texas, mother, was convicted of drowning her five children (2002).

- Nikolay Soltys, a father from the Ukraine, killed his wife and four children with a knife in Sacramento, California (2001).

- Dylan Klebold and Eric Harris murdered 12 fellow students and one teacher then themselves in Columbine High School, Littleton, Colorado (1999).

- A boy opened fire on a prayer meeting in Heath High School in Paducah, Kentucky, killing three and wounding five fellow students (1997).

George Barna's research says 85 percent of young people walk away from their faith when they leave their Christian parent's home.[1] You don't want your children included in that statistic. If your children know the Word of God and they learn to talk to God at an early age, you can prevent that from happening. Determine you'll be like Eunice, the mother of Timothy, who said of him, *"that from childhood you have known the Holy Scriptures…"* (2 Tim. 3:15).

It is dangerous to raise children today. There's an enemy of children, and it's not just a drug pusher or a killer. There is a spiritual enemy of children. *"…the devil walks about like a roaring lion, seeking whom he may devour"* (1 Pet. 5:8). While most adults can protect themselves in this life, what about the children?

Because children are defenseless, the enemy seems to target them more than any other age group. He pounces on them when they least expect it—and when adults are not around—to make them his prisoners. He would like to keep them in addiction for their entire natural life on earth, whether addiction to drugs, alcohol, pornography—anything to keep them in bondage.

While the devil is sneaking up on them, most of us don't know it. While he has several weapons in his arsenal, we don't know which ones he will use. While the devil will spring his attack at the right moment, we have no idea when it's coming or where. We appear to be completely helpless against such a wicked foe.

*Lord, protect my children from evil enemies
that I don't even know are attacking them.*

Many kids have heard the challenge several times from buddies, "My father can beat your father." That challenge is usually made in anger; most of us never saw fathers fighting. When Jesus dealt with the religious Pharisees, He called God, *"My Father"* (see John 5:17). To the Pharisees he said, *"Your father, the Devil"* (John 8:44). When God the Father fights against satan, the father of lies, it's spiritual warfare. That's a picture of the battle against your children.

What can we do when facing the drug dealer or the sex predator? While we can't humanly beat them, "Our Father (the Lord) can beat their father (the devil)." You need to rely on the promises, *"Greater is he that is in you, than he that is in the world"* (1 John 4:4 KJV).

*Lord, You are much greater in power than the devil. I
pray for You to stop his evil influence on my children.*

God uses people to help others; can He use you? Can God use you to make a difference in the lives of your children? Do you know what to pray and how to pray?

First, you must pray for them because intercession touches the heart of God. *"Pour out thine heart like water before the face of the Lord: lift up thy hands toward him for the life of thy young children"* (Lam. 2:19 KJV).

Lord, I will read and learn
to intercede for my children.

We want you to know how to pray for your children, or grand-child, niece, pupil in your Bible class, or a neighborhood child. We want you to know what it feels like to have God on your side.

You don't have to be a great spiritual prayer warrior for God to answer your prayers for children. The secret is God, not you. You don't get great answers because you're more spiritual than others or because you've prayed longer or better. No, not at all. The secret is God! The simplest prayer launched with the simplest faith can set the wheels of Heaven in motion. God can do all things. So the issue is God. Trust Him to do great things for your children.

Lord,
I know You love my children
and want them to be saved.
You also want to deliver them
from the evil one. So I pray
for You to guide me. I promise to do
everything within my power
to lead them to Christ and
train them in righteousness.
Help me keep my promise to
You and bless my child(ren). Amen.

We pray this book will change your life and your children, and the children of your children. May God use you to change the lives of your children as you pray for them to live according to His will for them.

Elmer Towns and David Earley
Written from our homes in sight
of the Blue Ridge Mountains

10

Endnote

1. Gordon Cloud cites George Barna statistics in The World From Our Window, August 2006, "Why Are Teens Leaving the Church?" http://theworldfrommywindow.blogspot.com/2006/08/survey-question-why-are-teens-leaving.html, (accessed 8 April 2009).

CHAPTER 1

Why Pray for Children?

Lord,
as I read this chapter, open my eyes and help me see
exactly what you have for me from these words.

Two Truths to Remember

1. *Never underestimate the challenges of parenting.* The journey of raising godly kids in an ungodly world is a relentless roller coaster of incredible heights and crushing depths. Joy and sorrow, laughter and tears, fun and frustration crash like waves on your heart through the events in the lives of your children. Fulfillment and fatigue, exhilaration and exhaustion are all part

of the process. Just when you think you have a handle on the challenges, your child hits another stage of development and the path is again clouded with fog.

Remember that there are no perfect children, no perfect parents, and no perfect parenting situation. Also, there are no two identical parenting situations. Every parent, every child, every family, and every child-raising situation is unique. We all need all the help we can get.

2. *Never underestimate the power of a praying parent.* There is hope! There is a living God who is supremely intelligent and infinitely powerful who already knows and loves you and your children more and better than you ever will. If you learn to cooperate with God in prayer for your children, He is able to do exceedingly, abundantly more than you can even ask or imagine.

Cathy and I (Dave Earley) have three sons. Nothing would bring us more joy than if they continue to love God passionately and serve Him fervently. Nothing would break our hearts more than if they veer off track and don't live for God.

Of course, our children are free moral agents and can choose to accept or reject our efforts in leading them to live for God, yet we believe with all our hearts that the more we pray for them, the more God works in their behalf. We also believe that the more accurately, biblically, and specifically we can pray for them, the more effectively God works in their hearts through the Word of God and their circumstances.

Ruth and I (Elmer Towns) believe the same way. Therefore, together we want to help you learn to pray more frequently, passionately, scripturally, and effectively for your children, no matter their ages. My children (Elmer) are already grown, so much of what I share in this book has passed the litmus test of personal and practical experience. I have learned the hard way what doesn't work and what shouldn't be done. We have a merciful Father who answers prayers and blesses children in spite of everything.

My sons (Dave) are all still in college. I base most of my teaching on the solid foundation of the Word of God.

Our prayer is that you will not just read this book. We want you to put everything you learn from it into practice. Our desire is that this book will direct and fuel your prayers, so you will know the great joy of seeing your children walk in truth (see 2 John 1:4; 3 John 1:3).

Dear Lord, lead our children to walk
in step with You as they walk in truth.

Praying for Children Makes a Difference

The Bible offers several examples of ordinary parents whose prayers produced extraordinary results in the lives of their children. Hannah prayed for a not-yet-conceived son. Her sincere, selfless, stubborn, sacrificial prayers resulted in the birth and life of the great prophet, Samuel (you can read their story in First Samuel 1-16).

A Canaanite mother found herself at wits end with her daughter. The poor girl was possessed by a demon. Nothing they tried helped. No one was able to bring relief. Yet that mother's persistent, resilient, faith-filled prayers brought about a miracle on behalf of her daughter (see Matt. 15:22-28).

The daughter of a government official had died. The simple, direct, faith-filled request of a father touched the heart of God and brought the girl back to life (see Matt. 9:18-28).

15

I have been privileged to know many godly pastors and missionaries. I am astounded at the number of godly men and women who, when asked for the secret of their spiritual success, point back to the persistent prayers of their parents. Praying for your children helps make a powerful, positive difference in their lives.

> # Prayer is powerful.

When I look at the massive responsibility of trying to influence my children for God, I am stunned by my own insufficiency. I can't do it. But I know someone who can—God. He can do more in seconds than I can accomplish in years. He can do it better, bigger, and more long-lastingly than I can even imagine.

So the question becomes, how can I somehow influence God to be more influential in the lives of my family? The answer, of course, is prayer.

Because prayer is active cooperation with God on behalf of your children, and because God is almighty, then prayer, in a sense, is omnipotent. Charles Spurgeon agreed. In speaking of prayer, he called it "the slender nerve that moves the muscles of omnipotence."[1] R.A. Torrey also agreed and made this astounding observation:

> Prayer is the key that unlocks all the storehouses of God's infinite grace and power. All that God is and all that God does is at the disposal of prayer. But we must use the key. Prayer can do anything God can do, and as God can do anything, prayer is omnipotent.[2]

Hudson Taylor discovered, "It is possible to move men through God by prayer alone."[3] I would add, it is also possible to move children through God by prayer alone.

In discussing the power of prayer, Jack Hayford observed:

You and I can help decide which of these two things—blessing or cursing—happens on earth. We determine whether God's goodness is released toward a specific situation or whether the sower of sin and Satan is permitted to prevail. Prayer is the determining factor... If we don't, He won't.[4]

God is omnipresent. Therefore, one of the amazing aspects of prayer is that, in a sense, it is also unlimited by space. Prayer invites God to work in our children's lives even when we can't be with them. *Prayer goes with your children when you can't.*

You can't be with your children 24 hours a day, every day, the rest of your life, nor should you want to be. But God can and will, if you pray. You can't go with your children to school, to work, to college, or when they get married. But God can and He will, as you pray. You can't be in two or more places at once, but God can and He will, when you pray.

> **Praying for your children is one of the best ways to love them.**

God gives us a burden, a holy concern for our children. We may not always accept their behavior, but we have a deep, genuine, almost inexplicable love for them.

Intercessory Prayer

One of the purest and most powerful ways for a parent to express and exercise such love is in intercessory prayer. "Love on its knees" is the definition and description Dick Eastman gives to intercessory prayer.[5] Such prayer seeks the best for our children before the throne of God and brings their needs to the One who has all of the answers. *Praying for children gives you necessary wisdom and insight.*

Children have the incredible power to get themselves tangled in situations that seem impossible to unravel. Raising them often brings you to the place of total bamboozlement and befuddlement. There are no easy answers or simple solutions. What can a parent do? Pray for wisdom.

James wrote to his spiritual children as they faced a variety of stiff trials and tribulations. Near the beginning of his letter he gave them an amazing promise:

> *If any of you lacks wisdom, he should ask God, who gives generously to all without finding fault, and it will be given to him* (James 1:5 NIV).

Praying for wisdom is a request God likes to answer.

Solomon is considered the wisest man who ever lived. When he assumed the spiritual responsibility for the "children of Israel" his response was to pray for wisdom.

Give me wisdom and knowledge, that I may lead this people, for who is able to govern this great people of yours? (2 Chronicles 1:10 NIV)

The content of Solomon's prayer should be a pattern for every spiritual father and mother.

Every parent, child, and situation is unique. Parenting is learned through on-the-job training and often involves sailing into unchartered waters. How do we know what to do next? Who has the answers? God does. Often, He reveals the insight we need only as we pray.

Lord, give me divine wisdom to pray
more effectively for my children.

No One Else Can Pray for Your Children Like You Can

The genuine love you have for your children, the tenderness you feel for them, and your knowledge of their make-up, needs, and problems, qualify you to plead with God on their behalf with an urgency and earnestness that will not be denied. Your love for your children fuels the power of your prayers on their behalf.

Also, it is comforting to realize that God is *our* heavenly *Father* as well as the heavenly *Father* of *our children*. When Jesus wanted to convince us of the Lord's willingness to hear prayer, He based his argument on the power of parental love:

If you then, being evil, know how to give good gifts to your children, how much more will your heavenly Father give the Holy Spirit to those who ask Him! (Luke 11:13)

> ## You are responsible for praying for your children.

It is your responsibility to pray for your children. Yes, it is great if a pastor, youth worker, Sunday school teacher, grandparent, uncle or aunt, or friend prays for your children. But the responsibility begins and ends with you. God tells parents, especially fathers, that they are the ones accountable for the spiritual development of their kids. Although it is not explicitly noted in these verses, praying for your children's spiritual development is clearly implied.

> *These commandments that I give you today are to be upon your hearts. Impress them on your children. Talk about them when you sit at home and when you walk along the road, when you lie down and when you get up. Tie them as symbols on your hands and bind them on your foreheads. Write them on the doorframes of your houses and on your gates* (Deuteronomy 6:6-9 NIV).

> *Fathers, do not exasperate your children; instead, bring them up in the training and instruction of the Lord* (Ephesians 6:4 NIV).

The great spiritual leader, Samuel, understood the severity of the responsibility of praying for his spiritual children. In fact he considered failing to do so a sin.

> *As for me, far be it from me that I should sin against the Lord by failing to pray for you. And I will teach you the way that is good and right* (1 Samuel 12:23 NIV).

If failing to pray for spiritual children is a sin, how much is it a sin to fail to pray for our biological children!

20

Lord,
forgive me for the times I have been guilty
of worrying about my children when I should
have been seriously praying for them. Help
me begin today to pray for my children more
consistently than I have at any time in my life.

Pray Scripture for Your Children

We want to encourage you to not merely pray for your children, but to incorporate God's Word into your prayers. We have found greater confidence, power, insight, and encouragement as we have learned to pray the Scriptures for our children.

> **Praying Scriptures gives**
> **divine power to your prayers.**

When we pray for our children, our prayers need all of the power we can give them. No other book ever written has a fraction of the power of the Bible. Put another way, all of the books ever written put together cannot compare with the life-giving power of the Word of God. Therefore, God's Word infuses our prayers with power when we pray the Bible for our children.

For the word of God is living and powerful, and sharper than
any two-edged sword, piercing even to the division of soul and
spirit, and of joints and marrow, and is a discerner of the
thoughts and intents of the heart (Hebrews 4:12).

Lord,
help me learn to pray the Scriptures for my
children in such a way as to make a positive,
life-giving, powerful difference in their lives.

> **Praying Scriptures adds divine insight to your prayers.**

On more than one occasion I have been completely over-whelmed by what was going on in one of my children's lives. It is on those occasions that I have gone to God and asked for direction as to how to even pray for them. The Bible has been my guide for what and how to pray (see Chapter 6).

The Bible is God's Word. When we pray the Scriptures we are praying the words of God back to Him. He did not give us these words haphazardly or accidentally. The words of Scripture were given to guide us as people and parents.

Your word is a lamp to my feet and a light to my path (Psalm 119:105).

> **The Bible contains the words of our heavenly Father for His children.**

Our God is not only our *God*, He is also our heavenly *Father*. Every word of the Bible is written straight from the heart of the greatest Father in the universe to His children. When I pray the Bible I am linking my heart with God's heart in behalf of my children. On top of that, since my sons have each accepted Jesus as their Savior and Lord, I can confidently ask the heavenly Father to parent them.

> *Lord,*
> *show me what it is You are working to accomplish in*
> *the lives of my children and help me pray for that to be*
> *occurring in their lives. They are Your children. Please*
> *parent them, especially in times and in ways I can't.*

The Bible Is God's Checkbook

Charles Spurgeon was one of the leading lights of church history. Like other high-impact spiritual leaders, Spurgeon would tirelessly read the Bible, fearlessly claim God's promises, and quote them back to Him in prayer. In his book, *God's Checkbook: Daily Drawing on God's Treasury*, Spurgeon explains:

> A promise from God may very instructively be compared to a check payable to order. It is given to the believer with the view of bestowing upon him some good thing. It is not meant that he should read it over comfortably, and have done with it. No, he is to treat it as a reality as a man treats a check.[6]

Spurgeon implores us to accept the promise personally as one's own. After doing so, the believer must pray.

...he must believingly *present* the promise to the Lord, as a man presents a check at the counter of the bank. He must plead it by prayer, expecting to have it fulfilled.[7]

The Bible is full of divine promises. When we pray the Scriptures, we are bringing the power of God's promises into the lives of our children. *Praying the Bible is transacting business with God.*

Transacting Business With God

Hudson Taylor was an Englishman who left a very deep mark for God both in China and around the world. From nothing, he founded the China Inland Mission, which at his death included 205 mission stations with over 800 missionaries and 125,000 Chinese Christians. Read that sentence again slowly.

How did he do it?

What was his secret?

Taylor's son and daughter-in-law wrote a biography of Hudson's life interestingly titled *Hudson Taylor's Spiritual Secret.* In it they state that there was one secret of the great impact of Hudson's leadership.

He overcame difficulties such as few men have ever had to encounter, and left a work which years after his death is growing in extent and usefulness...largely as an outcome of this life, tens of thousands of souls [have been] won to Christ in previously unreached provinces...What was his secret?...the simple, profound secret of drawing for every need upon "the fathomless wealth of Christ."[8]

Where did Taylor learn this type of prayer life? The secret came from his mother and his sister. He was converted through their persistent, prevailing prayers. His sister committed to give herself in prayer until her brother gave himself to Christ. The day she made her commitment, she wrote in her diary these words:

> The promises of the Bible are very real, and prayer is in a sober fact *transacting business with God,* whether on one's behalf or on the behalf of those whom one seeks blessing[9] (emphasis added).

"Transacting business" with God became a model for Taylor's dynamic life of bold faith and prayer. Every need, whether it was for his family, funds, converts, or workers came by trusting God and claiming His promises.

> **The Bible contains the words that others prayed for their spiritual children.**

As we will begin to explore in the next chapter, you will see that the Bible records the very words others, including Jesus and Paul, offered for their disciples. I have had great joy in praying these prayers for my three little disciples. I reason that if anyone knew how to pray for their disciples it was Jesus and Paul, so there is certainly nothing to lose and much to gain by praying the prayers they prayed.

The Bible also contains examples other parents effectively offered for their children. If God answered the petitions of those parents, He might do the same for me if I ask the same things for my children.

Now what? Suggestions for getting the most out of this book:

1. Study each chapter with an open heart. Ask God to speak to you as you read. Read with a pen in hand and underline the sentences that speak to you and your situation. Make notes in the margins.

2. Read this book with your spouse. Although there may be situations when doing so is impossible, if at all possible, read along with your mate and discuss how you can apply what you are learning.

3. Pray as you read. Within the text, we have included short sentence prayers when appropriate. Pause and pray those prayers as you read the book and you will get much more out of it.

4. Share what you are learning with someone else. If possible, study this book with a friend, several friends, as a small group, or Sunday school class. It will amaze you how much more you will get out of the book if you are discussing what you are learning and hearing with what others are learning.

5. Reread chapters as they apply to the needs in your life. Every time your children goes through a different stage in their physical, emotional, or spiritual development, you may want to read certain chapters of this book again because the applications and prayers you are praying will change.

6. Live what you learn. Don't merely read a book about praying for your children. Start now to pray for your children. Set aside time each day to pray for them— even if they are not yet born. Whisper prayers for them throughout the day. Get together with others

and pray for each other's children. Determine to pray for your children more often, more consistently, and more passionately than ever before.

Endnotes

1. Charles Spurgeon, *Twelve Sermons on Prayer* (Grand Rapids, MI: Baker Book House, 1971), 31.

2. R.A. Torrey, *The Power of Prayer* (Grand Rapids, MI: Zondervan, 1924), 17.

3. Hudson Taylor as quoted in J.O. Sanders, *Spiritual Leadership* (Chicago: Moody Press, 1974), 82.

4. Jack Hayford, *Prayer Is Invading the Impossible* (Orlando, FL: Bridge-Logos Publishers, 2002), Preface xxx.

5. Dick Eastman, *Love on Its Knees* (Grand Rapids, MI: Chosen Books, 1989), 56.

6. Charles Spurgeon, *God's Checkbook: Daily Drawing on God's Treasury* (Chicago: Moody Press, 1965), Preface ii.

7. Ibid.

8. Howard and Geraldine Taylor, *Hudson Taylor's Spiritual Secret* (Chicago: Moody Press, 1932), 14.

9. Ibid., 18.

Making the decision to have a child is momentous. It is to decide forever to have your heart go walking around outside your body.

—Elizabeth Stone

(http://www.quotegarden.com/parents.html)

I cannot tell how much I owe to the prayers of my good mother. I remember her once praying, "Now Lord, if my children go on in sin it will not be from ignorance that they perish, and my soul must bear swift witness against them at the day of judgment if they lay not hold on Christ and claim Him as their personal Savior."

—Charles Spurgeon

CHAPTER 2

How to Pray for Children
so God Answers

O Lord, teach me how to pray for
my children as effectively as possible.

Would you like to learn how to pray for your children in such a way that God answers and they benefit? Of course you would. The Bible gives two examples of mothers who saw wonderful answers as they prayed for their children. Let's learn from their examples.

The Prayer of Hannah for Her Future Son (1 Samuel 1:1-17)

Like all stories of great answers to prayer, this story begins with a great need. Hannah was a woman who deeply desired to have a baby. Sadly, she couldn't.

> *Now there was a certain man...and his name was Elkanah...And he had two wives: the name of one was Hannah, and the name of the other Peninnah. Peninnah had children, but Hannah had no children* (1 Samuel 1:1-2).

Note the lonely, desperate, painful words at the end of verse two, "Peninnah had children, but Hannah had no children." Hannah had no children in a world in which bearing children served as the chief source of a woman's esteem, provision, and protection. Her lifelong passion to be a mother went unfulfilled year after year.

> *This man went up from his city yearly to worship and sacrifice to the Lord of hosts in Shiloh...And whenever the time came for Elkanah to make an offering, he would give portions to Peninnah his wife and to all her sons and daughters. But to Hannah he would give a double portion, for he loved Hannah, although the Lord had closed her womb* (1 Samuel 1:3-5).

"*The Lord had closed her womb.*" Her barrenness was her burden. Because she had no child, Hannah felt worthless and unfulfilled. Certainly she tried all of the other mother's suggestions for how to get pregnant, but with no success. She was getting older. Her biological clock was running or had run out. Out of her desperation she crafted a prayer for a future son.

> *And she was in bitterness of soul, and prayed to the Lord and wept in anguish. Then she made a vow and said, "O Lord of*

32

hosts, if You will indeed look on the affliction of Your maidser-
vant and remember me, and not forget Your maidservant, but
will give Your maidservant a male child, then I will give him to
the Lord all the days of his life, and no razor shall come upon
his head" (1 Samuel 1:10-11).

Hannah cried out for a son. As you may already know, God answered her prayer "yes." But before we look at the answer to her prayer, it is insightful to notice a few of the characteristics of this prayer. Her prayer gives us a pattern for how to pray for our children so God will answer.

1. Surrender

If You will...not forget Your maidservant, but will give Your
maidservant a male child, then I will give him to the Lord all
the days of his life, and no razor shall come upon his head
(1 Samuel 1:11).

Hannah surrendered her future son to the Lord in prayer. One benefit of delayed answers is purified motives. The longer our dreams are heated in the flames of frustrating delay, the more the impurities in our motives are burnt off. Hannah had spiritual leverage to approach God in prayer for her son because she was willing to dedicate him to the Lord, no matter what. This produced a request that God could no longer deny.

Her future son was already dedicated to the Lord. If, or when, God should give her a son, she promised to "give him to the Lord." She wanted this to be a God-thing. God would be the giver and receiver of the son. The son would come from God and be returned to God. She merely wanted to have a part in the middle.

Her dream was deeper than holding a baby. It reached further than herself, her family, or even her village. It was for a son, given by God, given back to God, who could be used of God to influence a nation for God. So she cried out for a son.

If you want your prayers for your children to strike a chord with the heavenly Father, be certain that the child you pray for has been surrendered to Him. Like Hannah and Abraham much earlier, give that child to God.

Lord,
I dedicate and fully surrender my children to You.

2. Persistence

And it happened, as she continued praying before the Lord, that Eli watched her mouth (1 Samuel 1:12).

Hannah was stubbornly persistent in prayer. Her desperate desire was not merely offered to God once and forgotten. No. It was repeated over and over as she bared her soul before her God. She was shameless and stubborn. She was persistent and persevering—and eventually she prevailed. Her shameless stubborn persistence won out. Hannah prayed and did not give up. Her faith refused to yield until it was rewarded.

Most of us quit praying too easily and too quickly. The petitions that draw action are often the ones that we have poured out over and over again. Jesus promised that if we keep asking we will receive (see Matt. 7:7).

Lord,
help me be persistent in my prayers.

3. Passion

Now Hannah spoke in her heart; only her lips moved, but her voice was not heard. Therefore Eli thought she was drunk. So Eli said to her, "How long will you be drunk? Put your wine away from you!"

But Hannah answered and said, "No, my lord, I am a woman of sorrowful spirit. I have drunk neither wine nor intoxicating drink, but have poured out my soul before the Lord. Do not consider your maidservant a wicked woman, for out of the abundance of my complaint and grief I have spoken until now" (1 Samuel 1:13-16).

Hannah was supremely passionate in her prayers about a son. Hannah described herself as "a woman of sorrowful spirit." She was desperate. No one or nothing else would do—only God. The possibility of God not coming through was more than she could bear. So she poured her soul out to the Lord.

She was not merely pouring out words to the Lord. So deep was her desire that her voice was not even heard. She was pouring out her very soul as she prayed an extremely deep, highly personal, supremely passionate prayer.

She claimed to be praying "out of great anguish and grief." This prayer erupted from so deep within her soul that it hurt to let it out. It was born from an intensity that was beyond what words could utter.

There is something painful about exposing the subterranean reaches of our soul to God. To let down the drawbridge and allow our greatest dreams and passions to stand naked before God is threatening at best, and often agonizing. Yet this is what she did.

If we are lackadaisical in our praying, why should God be interested in responding? It is the passionate prayers that bring the most powerful answers. James promised that *"the effective, fervent prayer of a righteous man avails much"* (James 5:16).

35

Lord,
help me pray passionately for my children.

4. Sacrifice

...therefore she wept and did not eat. Then Eli answered and said, "Go in peace, and the God of Israel grant your petition which you have asked of Him." And she said, "Let your maid-servant find favor in your sight." So the woman went her way and ate, and her face was no longer sad (1 Samuel 1:7,17-18).

"She wept and did not eat," Hannah was sacrificial in her prayer. She did not eat until she was assured that she had broken through. Obviously, she had been abstaining from food as part of her prayer. She was either so determined that she would not eat or so distraught she could not eat; but either way, she was fasting.

As a parent, there are times when the needs of our children are greater than our need to eat. Some of the greatest break-throughs in the lives of my boys have come as a result of days of fasting and prayer on their behalf. That was the result for Hannah.

Then they rose early in the morning and worshiped before the Lord, and returned and came to their house at Ramah. And Elkanah knew Hannah his wife, and the Lord remembered her. So it came to pass in the process of time that Hannah conceived and bore a son, and called his name Samuel, saying, "Because I have asked for him from the Lord" (1 Samuel 1:19-20).

Hannah got her answer. God gave her a son, and what a son! Little Samuel became one of Israel's greatest prophets. He became a mighty man of prayer. His name, Samuel, meaning "God heard," was a constant reminder that God heard and answered his mother's prayer for her future son.

It Works!

I (Dave) have taught on Hannah's prayer for her future son at my church. As a result, barren women and couples have been moved to a deeper level in their prayers. Women "who couldn't get pregnant," found themselves pregnant. Couples were led to adopt precious babies in need of a home. Spiritual break-throughs occurred in the lives of children. Even some prodigals returned home.

A friend of mine, Rhonda, had had no contact with her adult daughter, Megan, for several years. A few years ago, Rhonda became part of our church and returned to God after a couple of decades of distance. Soon she discovered a renewed burden to connect with her daughter. One Sunday morning she heard a message on the Hannah prayer and the power of prayer with fasting. She had become desperate to see her daughter again after all the years of separation. At this point she realized she had nothing to lose, so she gave prayer and fasting a serious try.

She began her fast on Monday, eating nothing and drinking only water, determined to persistently and passionately seek God with desperate prayer on behalf of Megan. On Thursday evening she got a phone call.

It was Megan.

After all those years, she had felt an overwhelming urge to get back together with her mom. God had heard Rhonda's prayer for her prodigal daughter.

But that's not all Rhonda prayed about. She began to pray about Megan's spiritual condition. Soon Megan began coming to church with her mom and recently trusted Christ as her Savior.

The Prayer of the Canaanite Woman for Her Daughter (Matthew 15:21-28)

No one on earth has the power to break your heart like your own children. Seeing them hurt and watching them struggle is a gut-wrenching, soul-shaking experience. You feel their pain. They have the power in a split second to bring tears of incredible joy and pride to your eyes. But they can also so deeply disappoint you that it feels like a knife jabbed directly into your heart. When they are treated unjustly, righteous indignation can overwhelm your common sense. When they hurt, you would do anything you could to take their place.

As parents, sometimes the need is greater than our resources. We feel desperate. There is a very special prayer that is the cry of a desperate parent. It is found in Matthew 15 as we see Jesus resting from his heavy schedule in a non-Jewish region east of the Mediterranean Sea. Here He encountered a desperate mom.

1. Petition

> *Then Jesus went out from there and departed to the region of Tyre and Sidon. And behold, a woman of Canaan came from that region and cried out to Him, saying, "Have mercy on me, O Lord, Son of David! My daughter is severely demon-possessed"* (Matthew 15:21-22).

The mother took her overwhelming problem to Jesus. She cried out to Him for mercy. While there is much we don't fully understand about demon possession, we do know that it has gruesome physical results and emotional expressions. We recognize that those possessed by the evil one experience severe pain. Human medicines may relieve symptoms but they are ineffective to produce lasting cures. Modern psychology wrestles to adequately understand, explain, or deal with it.

We also know that it must have been absolutely devastating for this mother to see her daughter in such awful anguish of the soul. So she cried out to Jesus for mercy.

Yet, her first request was ineffective.

But He answered her not a word... (Matthew 15:23).

2. Perseverance

As a follower of Jesus, I find it most difficult to deal with the unexplained silences of God. We have all been there. There is a legitimate need. You come to the Lord for mercy. But all you get in response is the deafening silence of God. Most people quit at this point.

This woman, a Canaanite, was used to the unresponsiveness of praying to her gods. This was not new to her. She could have easily marked Jesus down to be just as uncaring or impotent as her gods. But she didn't. She persevered in crying out to Jesus for help.

...And His disciples came and urged Him, saying, "Send her away, for she cries out after us" (Matthew 15:23).

She refused to give up easily or go quietly. She kept coming. Her pain was greater than her pride. So she persisted, and Jesus finally responded.

But He answered and said, "I was not sent except to the lost sheep of the house of Israel" (Matthew 15:24).

Lord, help me not get discouraged
and quit as I pray for my children.

39

3. Pleading

Ouch! Jesus did not even speak directly to her. He made his comment to His disciples. It certainly was not what she hoped He would say.

But she refused to be denied. She knew that she had no right to ask a Jewish man to help her. She knew that she had no basis for expecting Him to respond. But she had heard that He was mighty and compassionate. Her daughter was in extreme need. She had no choice, so she pressed the issue ahead.

Then she came and worshiped Him, saying, "Lord, help me!" (Matthew 15:25).

With all of her faith, all of her emotions, and all of her love for her daughter, she pleaded. The weight of her need, every ounce of her hurt, and the totality of her helplessness were embodied in those three little words, "Lord, help me."

How do you pray when you don't know what to pray? What words can better express the burden of the broken-hearted parent? "Lord, help me."

But He answered and said, "It is not good to take the children's bread and throw it to the little dogs" (Matthew 15:26).

4. Prevailing

Yet again her prayer goes without a response. But this heroic mother had the heart of a lion when it came to prayer for her daughter. She would not be denied.

And she said, "Yes, Lord, yet even the little dogs eat the crumbs which fall from their masters' table" (Matthew 15:27).

"Yes, Lord, yet..." This mom was not going to give up until Jesus did something for her daughter. She would not take "no" as the final answer. Her persistent faith cracked the wall of unwillingness she encountered in the ways of the Almighty. Finally, Jesus did something.

> *Then Jesus answered and said to her, "O woman, great is your faith! Let it be to you as you desire." And her daughter was healed from that very hour* (Matthew 15:28).

How do we pray for our children so the Lord answers?

Like this mother, we must have great faith. Jesus commended her on her great faith. A look back through this passage reveals the greatness of her faith. She was a Canaanite, a non-Jew, a not yet fully devoted follower of Jesus. For her to come so openly to Jesus for help shows that she had great faith considering the small amount of truth and light she had received in her life. She had not had the privilege of growing up hearing about the powerful love of the God of the Bible. For her to come to Jesus meant that she had to turn from pagan deities and familiar gods to trust Him to help her. Her faith was great for someone from her background. Coming to Jesus, persistently asking and not giving up until she was helped, took all of the faith she had.

Her faith was great because it was not based on a sense of her own merit, wisdom, or strength. It was based completely on her strong conviction that Jesus was able and willing to help those in need. She positioned herself as a dog seeking crumbs from its master.

> *Lord, I believe that you are willing and*
> *able to work on behalf of my children.*
> *I will keep on asking until I receive.*

It Works!

Two of our children (Dave) suffer from bipolar disorder. The chemicals in their brain misfire in such a way as to make them very easily susceptible to depression and anxiety. A few years ago one of them was struggling mightily to function because of severe social anxiety while at the same time another was practically paralyzed by depression. Our daily prayers were just not getting the job done on their behalf.

We were scared because we felt like we had in many ways "lost" our sons. It seemed as if they may never reach their full potential in Christ. We were desperate and nearly defeated.

I determined to spend a week fasting and praying like Hannah and persistently pleading their case to the Lord as did the Canaanite mother. Again and again, over and over, I cried out to God to "Show them mercy" and to "Help us." I pleaded with Him to "Give us our sons back."

After a week, nothing seemed to change, but I did not feel called to continue fasting.

Slowly God worked. Little by little they got better and were functioning in their college studies. Today both are doing great, serving the Lord, and studying to be pastors!

Your Turn

Both Hannah and the Canaanite mother were granted glorious answers to their prayers. Hannah received a son. The Canaanite mother saw her daughter healed. Hannah showed us that the Lord responds to a parent's prayers when they surrender their children to the Lord, are stubbornly persistent, supremely passionate, and sacrificial in their prayers. The Canaanite mother taught us that prayer is most effective for our children when it is an expression of all the faith we have, refuses to quit, and humbly pleads to the Lord.

Read slowly through the following list and ask yourself which of these practices you need to take into your own prayers for your children.

1. I have fully surrendered my child/children to the Lord.

2. I am stubbornly persistent in my prayers on their behalf.

3. I pour out my heart to the Lord in prayer for my children.

4. I will sacrifice food (fast) or other things in order to pray most effectively for my children.

5. I pray for my children with as much faith as I can possibly express.

6. I refuse to quit until the Lord responds.

7. I keep praying because I know I don't have all the answers, but the Lord does. He is willing and able to answer.

*Lord, I give my children to serve You
however You see fit, wherever You desire,
whenever You wish. There are times when
I have no idea how to parent, what to say,
what to do or where to turn. Help me.*

If I had my child to raise all over again,
I'd build self-esteem first, and the house later.
I'd finger-paint more, and point the finger less.
I would do less correcting and more connecting. I'd take my
eyes off my watch, and watch with my eyes. I'd take more
hikes and fly more kites. I'd stop playing serious, and serious-
ly play. I would run through more fields and gaze at more
stars. I'd do more hugging and less tugging.

—Diane Loomans
from "If I Had My Child To Raise Over Again"
(http://www.quotegarden.com/parents.html)

If a child lives with criticism,

he learns to condemn.

If a child lives with hostility,

he learns to fight.

If a child lives with shame,

he learns to feel guilty.

If a child lives with tolerance,

he learns to be patient.

If a child lives with ridicule,

he learns to be shy.

If a child lives with encouragement,

he learns confidence.

If a child lives with fairness,

he learns justice.

If a child lives with security,

he learns to have faith.

If a child lives with approval,

he learns to like himself.

If a child lives with acceptance and friendship,
he learns to find love in the world.

Author Unknown

(http://www.nyssf.org/quotes.html)

CHAPTER 3

Praying With Jesus for Children

Dear Lord,
teach me to pray like Jesus for my children.

Would you pray for your children more if you were confident that what you were praying for them aligned with God's desires for their lives? Sure you would.

Maybe you are like I (Dave) was when our first son was born. I was very willing *to* pray for my child, but was not exactly sure *what* to say when I prayed.

Who better to model our prayers after than Jesus? Although He was not the biological father of children, He clearly served as a spiritual father to the men we call "the disciples." As their rabbi,

He was teacher, counselor, mentor, trainer, and leader whose task it was to raise up His followers to the point of being able to replicate His life and teachings to become the next generation of followers of the Law of God.

In many ways, Christian parents have a similar set of roles and responsibilities. We must teach, counsel, mentor, train, and lead our children. Our job is to raise up our children to become the next generation of Christ followers. Clearly the role Jesus played in the lives of His disciples is very similar to the role we have as the parents of our children. Therefore, we can confidently take the prayers He prayed for them and apply them to our situations as we pray for our children.

The John 17 "High Priestly" Prayer of Jesus for His Disciples (John 17:13-17)

John 17:13-17 contains the final discourses Jesus gave before His death, burial, and resurrection. As such, these chapters contain some of the greatest words of comfort, instruction, and prediction ever given. John 17 is the consummation of His dissertation. This farewell prayer for His disciples is the longest recorded prayer of Jesus. In it He prays for Himself (John 17:1-5), His current disciples (John 17:6-19), and those who would follow in the future, including us and our children (John 17:20-26). This prayer focuses on three primary requests.

1. Glorification

Before we look at the five requests He offers for His spiritual children, we should note the basis and context of the petitions for the disciples was Jesus' own request that the Father would glorify Him.

Jesus spoke these words, lifted up His eyes to heaven, and said: "Father, the hour has come. Glorify Your Son, that Your Son also may glorify You. And now, O Father, glorify Me together with Yourself, with the glory which I had with You before the world was" (John 17:1,5).

Jesus was hours away from going to the Cross to die for our sins. When Jesus asked the Father to glorify Him, it was not a selfish request. Jesus wanted the glory that would come from the immense love, vast power, and infinite wisdom of God that was about to be revealed through the work of salvation to ultimately reflect back on the Father. What this means to us is that we should condition all of our praying for our children with the passionate desire that the result of these requests always point back to reflect not our glory as parents, but glory to God. Too often parents pray that their children will do well so that the parents will look good. No. We should pray that our children do well so God is glorified.

Lord, please help my children live in such a way as to bring You the greatest glory.

2. Protection

I have given them Your word; and the world has hated them because they are not of the world, just as I am not of the world. "I do not pray that You should take them out of the world, but that You should keep them from the evil one. They are not of the world, just as I am not of the world. Sanctify them by Your truth. Your word is truth. As You sent Me into the world, I also have sent them into the world" (John 17:14-18).

There are several truths we can learn from this prayer. *First, Jesus did not ask God to remove His followers from the world.* The concept

49

of "the world" as used most frequently in the Scriptures describes the fallen system of society that is dominated by *"the lust of the flesh, the lust of the eyes, and the pride of life"* (1 John 2:15-17). It is like a river guided by the enemy that naturally flows away from God. It is fallen, corrupted, and will eventually pass away.

Jesus knew that because of Him, His followers would face intense hatred from the world. Therefore, we could assume that His request would be that God would take them out of the world. But nothing could be further from the truth. Instead, Jesus said, "I do not pray that You should take them out of the world, but that You should keep them from the evil one."

Too often, well-meaning parents try to overprotect their children by attempting to take them out of the world. Yet, this tactic does not work, as the world is a system not a place. When the child gets out from under their parents' protection, they often run headlong into the world, their curiosity being their downfall.

Second, Jesus sent His followers into the world. He said, *"As You sent Me into the world, I also have sent them into the world"* (John 17:18). Later He would commission them for ministry with the words, *"As the Father has sent Me, I also send you"* (John 20:21). Nowhere in the Bible did Jesus express the desire that His children were to totally isolate themselves from the world. He told us that as salt we were to get out of our salt shakers, and as light we were to shine among men (see Matt. 5:13-16). Jesus sent His followers into the world.

Prior to third grade, we (Dave and Cathy) educated our children at home in order to instill a love for reading and for the Lord. In third grade we felt they were ready, so we put them in a public school with the message, "You will either be a missionary, or you will quickly become a mission field." For the most part they were effective missionaries who led many of their schoolmates to Christ. In middle school they led Bible studies on campus before school on Thursday mornings. In high school they helped lead a Wednesday night home Bible study where many of their friends came to Christ. As a result of "being in the world, but not of it," they learned to defend their faith, gained a passion for the lost, and developed a deep desire to reach them. As mentioned previously, two of our sons are currently studying to be pastors.

In our church at that time, there were several families who severely criticized us for "sending our children into the world" instead of homeschooling them all the way through. It is interesting to note that in those families that tried to keep their children from the world, the opposite occurred. When they were old enough to get some freedom, many of the children dove headlong into the world. Only a few are still walking with the Lord. Understand the issue was not so much a matter of homeschool versus public school (or Christian school for that matter). The issue was one of motivation.

Third, Jesus did not pray His spiritual children to be removed from the world, *but that they would be protected from the evil one.* One of the 12 disciples, Judas, had already surrendered to the power of the evil one (see John 13:27). As you recall, Jesus had taught the disciples to pray for each other that the Father would "deliver them from the evil one" (Matt. 6:13). Like Jesus, we should pray for the spiritual, mental, emotional, and physical safe-keeping of our children as they live in a fallen, crooked world. Even when satan may attack their bodies, may he be unable to get their hearts.

Lord, as my children go into the world,
please protect them from the evil one.

3. Sanctification

Sanctify them by Your truth. Your word is truth (John 17:17).

There are several truths we can learn from this prayer. *First, Jesus' second request flowed from the first.* Jesus had prayed that the Father would not remove them from the world, but protect them from the evil one. Now He prays that they would become more holy in the process. The word *sanctify* is from the root word for "holy." It means separate from sin and separate to God. It describes a person who in heart, mind, thought, words, and actions is avoiding sin and drawing closer to God. When we pray this prayer for our children, we are asking God the Holy Spirit to work in the lives of our children to make them more holy.

Second, Jesus said that sanctification is the product of truth. One is sanctified only to the extent that they are governed by the truth. The truth is revealed in Jesus Christ and is found in His Word. When Jesus gave these words, He would soon no longer be personally available to them as He had been the previous three years. From now on their lives would need to be governed by His Word.

When we pray this prayer for our children we are asking God to open their eyes to see wonderful truth in His Word (see Ps. 119:18); to motivate them to be doers of the Word and not hearers only (see James 1:21-22); and to use His inspired Word to reprove, rebuke, correct, and instruct them in righteousness that they may be fully equipped for every good work (see 2 Tim. 3:16-17).

Praying With Jesus for Your Children

- Glorification: *My heavenly Father, the ultimate goal of all of my prayers on behalf of my children is that You would glorify Yourself in them.*

- Protection: *I ask, that You would not remove them from the world, but send them into it as missionaries. As You do, please protect them from the evil one.*

- Sanctification: Please make them more holy. Use Your word to sanctify their lives.

The Prayer of Jesus for Peter
(Luke 22:31-32)

On the night He was betrayed, Jesus had many extremely important things He needed to tell His spiritual children so they would be prepared for all that was about to occur. As He washed their feet, as they shared a final meal together, as they walked across the Kidron Valley and into the Mount of Olives, Jesus made the most significant statements of His earthly life. He knew that soon He would be arrested, tried, whipped, crucified, buried, and resurrected. By the end of that weekend, His relationship with His followers would be forever altered. They would have to stand on their own. He was leaving, and they would need to be ready to assume the immense human responsibility for advancing the Kingdom of God.

In the sense of a child entering the doorway of independence, the importance of what was said that night was similar to the conversation a dad may have with his son the night before he is to enlist in the Army or a mom with her daughter the night before her wedding.

What is highly interesting about His last evening talk is a short comment Jesus made specifically to Peter. These two short sentences are often overlooked, as they are only recorded in one of the four Gospels. Yet to those of us looking for insights into how to most effectively pray for our children, they stand out and shine like buried treasure.

> *And the Lord said, "Simon, Simon! Indeed, Satan has asked for you, that he may sift you as wheat. But I have prayed for you, that your faith should not fail; and when you have returned to Me, strengthen your brethren"* (Luke 22:31-32).

Think of it. Jesus told Peter *that* He was praying for him and exactly *what* He was praying for him. His words can encourage us to pray for our children and provide us with a pattern we can use to pray for our children. Before we look at the content of this prayer, note several insights:

First, Jesus referred to him by his given name "Simon," instead of the nickname "Peter" (the rock). Why? Probably to signify the fact that in himself, apart from Christ, Simon was weak and susceptible to temptation.

Second, Jesus began, "Simon, Simon." Why? The repetition indicates emphasis and deep concern. What is about to be shared is very serious information.

Third, Jesus said, "Satan desired to sift you as wheat." What does that mean? Sifting wheat refers to the swift, violent, repeated shaking of wheat in a sieve in which the grain drops to the bottom and the chaff rises to the top to be blown away. Jesus is warning Peter that satan would hit him with swift, severe, repeated temptation with the goal of separating Peter from Jesus. As we know, Peter was tempted three times to deny Jesus. Interestingly, while Jesus is speaking specifically to Peter, He uses a plural sense of the word "you" to indicate that satan will face severe testing.

Parents, let me remind you that we are in a spiritual war that must be taken seriously. Satan wants to hit your child with such sudden, severe, and successive temptation and testing that the child will turn from God.

Fourth, Jesus said, "But, I have prayed for you." Even though satan would attack, Jesus had prayed. Jesus is saying that He was covering them in general, and Peter in particular, in prayer. He had prayed that night and probably many times previously. Parents, we must let this word from Jesus spur us to pray for our children.

In this prayer of Jesus for Peter we see two significant requests that we can pray for our children.

4. Prevailing Faith

First, Jesus told Peter, *"I have prayed for you that your faith should not fail."* Initially, we might assume that Jesus is praying that Peter would not yield to temptation, but if we have read the rest of the story we know that Peter did yield to temptation and did deny the Lord three times. Plus, the next phrase gives it away when Jesus says, "and when you have returned to Me." Jesus is assuming that Peter would get off track, even if only briefly. Therefore, we can assume that the essence of this request is that even though Peter might get knocked down, he would get back up. Ultimately his faith would prevail.

As our children get older we cannot shield them from every time and type of testing, nor should we. They will never successfully make the trek to independence from us and dependence on Christ without learning to weather the attacks and the appeals of the enemy. Sometimes they will win and sometimes they will stumble and fall. We need to pray that when tested they will not give in, but even when they fall, they will get back up and keep going for God. Sometimes they will get off track. We need to pray that those times are brief and that they will retrace their steps back to the Lord. As Jesus prayed for Peter, we need to pray that our children will learn from their mistakes to depend more completely on the Lord.

Recently one of my sons (Dave) was hit with a severe and sudden temptation. He was already exhausted from lack of sleep and the test completely overwhelmed him. Unfortunately before he knew it, he yielded, and apart from the grace of God the consequences could have been severe to the point of being life-threatening. It could have been a giant mess. Interestingly, that very morning I had happened to pray for him this prayer for prevailing faith. At the time, I, of course, had no idea how applicable it would be. Fortunately the Lord answered my request. His stumble resulted in minimal damage but maximum life change. He quickly got back up and got going harder for God than before. But this time even more keenly aware of his need to rely on the Lord.

5. Resulting Ministry

The second part of Jesus' request for Peter is also very applicable for us. He told Peter that He prayed, "When you have returned to *Me*, strengthen your brethren." Jesus' request was that Peter would use his fall in order to better minister to others. God answered that petition. Read the Book of Acts and you will see how much the Lord was able to use Peter to bless others. In the face of great opposition and persecution, Peter became the leader of the first and largest church in the world at that time. Can you imagine how arrogant Peter might have become with such "success" if he had not yielded to temptation that night? God could have never used him.

I have found that every time I go through a difficult experience, I gain a key of ministry effectiveness that unlocks people's hearts. People connect much more easily with our failures than with our successes. We need to pray that even when our children stumble and fall, they would not only get back up, but they would use the lessons they learned to better serve and minster to others.

Prayer Requests for Your Children

• Prevailing Faith

Heavenly Father, when my children are tested, may their faith not give in or give up. Keep them from stumbling. But if and when they stumble, may they get back up and keep going toward You and for You.

• Resulting Ministry

May they use everything they experience—good and bad—to better minister to others.

Jesus Prays

Mark's Gospel records a sample 24-hour time period in the life of Jesus. Its dizzying level of activity rivals one of a mother with several small children at home. In the span of 24 hours, Jesus gave an amazing teaching at the synagogue (see Mark 1:21-22), cast a violent, belligerent demon out of a man (see Mark 1:23-28), and healed Simon Peter's mother so she could fix Jesus and His disciples lunch (see Mark 1:29-31). He then spent the rest of the day and late into the night healing sick people and casting demons out of the terrorized (see Mark 1:32-34). Whew!

It's hard to imagine a more draining day. If He was like many of us after such a draining day, the next morning might have been spent sleeping in and chilling out. But Jesus had a deep capacity for ministry because He practiced a few holy habits that yielded powerful results.

Was Jesus sleeping in the next day? No. Read verse 35 carefully.

Now in the morning, having risen a long while before daylight, He went out and departed to a solitary place; and there He prayed (Mark 1:35).

Note that Jesus had a specific *time* for prayer (in the morning) and a specific *place* for prayer (a solitary place). I have been training people in the area of prayer for 30 years. Again and again, I have found that if they will select a time and place for prayer, they are halfway home in developing a powerful prayer life.

> ### Jesus set aside a specific time and place to pray.

Determine a set time each day when you will pray for your children. It could be first thing in the morning or last thing at night. Some do it over their lunch hour. The right time is the time that works for you.

Select a place for prayer. We read in Mark about Jesus going out to a "quiet place." In Matthew, Jesus mentions going into your room and closing the door—*"when you pray, go into your room, and when you have shut your door, pray to your Father who is in the secret place; and your Father who sees in secret will reward you openly"* (see Matt. 6:1-15). Your place could be at a desk or the kitchen table or kneeling beside your bed or in the car on the way to work. I often enjoy taking a prayer walk in the middle of the day. The right place is the place that is right for you.

Try to pray a set amount of time for your children each day. Susanna Wesley was the mother of 19 children. Imagine the chaos in a home with so many children and an often absentee husband! Her goal was to spend one hour in prayer for her children each day. When Susanna wanted to spend time with God, she had a unique way of finding her "quiet" place. She would sit down in her kitchen and pull her apron up over her head. She would then spend time in prayer and the children knew not to disturb her! Her prayers made an impact. Her sons John and Charles later led the great evangelical awakening of the eighteenth century in England and founded the Methodist church. Of his mother's prayers, John wrote, "I learned more about Christianity from my mother than from all the theologians of England."[1]

There are 24 hours in a day or 1440 minutes. Setting aside 15, 30, or 60 minutes a day to pray for your children may be the best investment of your time you could possibly make.

Your Turn

Which of these prayers from Jesus do you need to especially focus on as you pray for your children?

1. Glorification

Heavenly Father, the ultimate goal of all of my prayers in behalf of my children is that You would glorify Yourself in them.

2. Protection

> *I ask, that You would not remove them from the world, but send them into it as missionaries. As You do, please protect them from the evil one.*

3. Sanctification

> *Please make them more holy. Use Your word to sanctify their lives.*

4. Prevailing Faith

> *Heavenly Father, when my children are tested, may their faith not give in or give up. Keep them from stumbling. But if and when they stumble, may they get back up and keep going toward You and for You.*

5. Resulting Ministry

> *May they use everything they experience—good and bad—to better minister to others.*

When and where will you pray each day?

1. My time(s):

2. My amount of time:

3. My place:

Endnote

1. John Wesley, http://www.anchoryourlife.com/prayer/wesley.html, (accessed 20 April 2009).

It behooves a father to be blameless
if he expects his child to be.

Homer

(http://www.quotegarden.com/parents.html)

*Jesus called a little child to him and put the child
among them. Then he said, "I tell you the truth,
unless you turn from your sins and become like little children,
you will never get into the Kingdom of Heaven. So anyone who
becomes as humble as this
little child is the greatest in the Kingdom of Heaven. And anyone who welcomes a little child like this on
my behalf is welcoming me. But if you cause one of these little
ones who trusts in me to fall into sin, it would
be better for you to have a large millstone tied around your neck
and be drowned in the depths of the sea"*
(Matthew 18:2-6 NLT).

*One day some parents brought their children to Jesus
so he could lay his hands on them and pray for them. But the
disciples scolded the parents for bothering him. But Jesus said,
"Let the children come to me. Don't stop them! For the Kingdom
of Heaven belongs to those who are like these children"*
(Matthew 19:13-14 NLT).

CHAPTER 4

Praying With Paul for Children

*O Lord, I thank You for the life and ministry
of Paul. Just as he had many follow his
faith, may my children follow my faith.*

The apostle Paul was an outstanding spiritual father for young Christians in the many churches he started (see 1 Cor. 4:14-16; 1 Thess. 2:11). The role of spiritual parent was one he took very seriously as he taught, modeled, encouraged, and especially prayed for his spiritual children. Fortunately for us, he recorded many of the prayers he regularly offered on behalf of his spiritual children. From those prayers we learn a great deal about how we can pray for children.

In one sitting, I (Dave) read the content of each of Paul's prayers in four translations. Wow! Reading them all at once shook me, convicted me, challenged me, and powerfully encouraged me as I pray for my children.

Paul's prayers are found in the following Scripture passages:

Romans 1:8-10; 15:5-6,13

Ephesians 1:15-19, 3:14-19

Philippians 1:9-11

Colossians 1:9-12

1 Thessalonians 1:2-3; 3:11-13

2 Thessalonians 1:11-12

Philemon 1:4-6

Before we look at each of the prayers separately, let's look at them as a group. In doing so, we can learn several powerful insights into how to most effectively pray for our children.

Paul's Keys to Effective Intercession

Consistency

The first thing that jumps out as you study Paul's prayers is his repeated mention of how consistently and constantly he prayed for them. Obviously Paul viewed regular, consistent, frequent, fervent, constant prayer as a primary responsibility he held for his spiritual children.

Romans 1:9: *"...without ceasing I make mention of you always in my prayers."*

64

Ephesians 1:16: *"Do not cease to give thanks for you, making mention of you in my prayers."*

Colossians 1:3: *"...praying always for you."*

1 Thessalonians 1:2-3: *"We give thanks to God always for you all, making mention of you in our prayers, remembering without ceasing...."*

1 Thessalonians 3:10: *"Night and day praying exceedingly...."*

2 Thessalonians 1:11: *"We also pray always for you...."*

2 Timothy 1:3: *"...without ceasing I remember you in my prayers night and day."*

Philemon 1:4: *"I thank my God, making mention of you always in my prayers."*

Look back through these verses and observe the drumbeat repetition describing the consistency of Paul's prayers for his spiritual children—"without ceasing," "always," "do not cease," "always," "without ceasing," "night and day," "exceedingly," "always," "without ceasing," "day and night," "always." You get the idea that he never missed a day, let alone an opportunity, to pray for his spiritual children. Every time they came to mind, he offered a prayer on their behalf.

Maybe you are like me. I will pray much when there are emergencies or crises, but I tend to slack off when the pressure lets off. I need to learn to pray consistently even when there is no crisis. If I did, maybe there would be fewer crises.

Often we think about our children, talk about our children, even spend time with our children, but how much time do we actually spend praying for them? I would guess that most of us would have to say that the frequency of our prayers is too little, too rare, and often too late. As mentioned previously, I strongly encourage you to have a set time, at least once a day when you pray Scripture for your children.

Lord, help me pray more often, more
consistently, more continually for my children.

Gratitude

Paul was not only consistent in his prayers, but he was constant in his gratitude. Again and again he mentions how thankful he is for his spiritual children and the work God had already done and was doing in them. Read these verses and note Paul's heartbeat of gratitude.

Romans 1:8 (NIV) *"First, I **thank** my God through Jesus Christ for all of you, because your faith is being reported all over the world."*

1 Corinthians 1:4-7 *"I **thank** my God always concerning you for the grace of God which was given to you by Christ Jesus, that you were enriched in everything by Him in all utterance and all knowledge, even as the testimony of Christ was confirmed in you, so that you come short in no gift...."*

Ephesians 1:15-16 *"...after I heard of your faith in the Lord Jesus and your love for all the saints, do not cease to give **thanks** for you...."*

Philippians 1:3-6 *"I **thank** my God upon every remembrance of you, always in every prayer of mine making request for you all with joy, for your fellowship in the gospel from the first day until now, being confident of this very thing, that He who has begun a good work in you will complete it until the day of Jesus Christ."*

Colossians 1:3-4 *"We give **thanks** to the God and Father of our Lord Jesus Christ, praying always for you, since we heard of your faith in Christ Jesus and of your love for all the saints."*

1 Thessalonians 1:2-3 *"We give **thanks** to God always for you all, making mention of you in our prayers, remembering without ceasing your work of faith, labor of love, and patience of hope in our Lord Jesus Christ in the sight of our God and Father."*

1 Thessalonians 2:13 *"For this reason we also **thank** God without ceasing, because when you received the word of God which you heard from us, you welcomed it not as the word of men, but as it is in truth, the word of God, which also effectively works in you who believe."*

1 Thessalonians 3:9 *"For what **thanks** can we render to God for you, for all the joy with which we rejoice for your sake before our God."*

2 Thessalonians 1:3 *"We are bound to **thank** God always for you, brethren, as it is fitting, because your faith grows exceedingly, and the love of every one of you all abounds toward each other."*

2 Timothy 1:3-5 *"I **thank** God, whom I serve with a pure conscience, as my forefathers did, as without ceasing I remember you in my prayers night and day...when I call to remembrance the genuine faith that is in you...."*

Philemon 1:4-5 *"I **thank** my God, making mention of you always in my prayers, hearing of your love and faith which you have toward the Lord Jesus and toward all the saints."*

Do you thank God for your children every day? Or are you like I am, often taking for granted that God has given them to you as a gift, taking for granted that He has already been working in their lives? We should learn from Paul to spend time each day thanking God for our children.

Parenting can be the most discouraging task we ever face. Some of our children go through stretches when it is at best three steps forward, two steps back. Paul spiritually parented Christians who could have worn him out and driven him crazy. But they did not make him bitter, cynical, or discouraged. Why? He always thanked God for them. What I find challenging is that he was not only thankful for the famous faith of the Romans and the amazingly influential Thessalonians, but he was also grateful for the Corinthians. His Corinthian children were always struggling to follow his leadership. They continually fought with each other. They got off track easily, quickly, and often.

We should note not only *that* Paul was grateful, but also for *what* he was grateful. He did not mention thanks for their good health or easy lives. Instead, he was grateful to God for what He had done in their lives, what He was doing in their lives, and what He would do in their lives. Paul's base of gratitude was spiritual, not physical or material. I am not saying that we should not thank God for the physical, material, educational, and vocational blessings He gives our children. But the primary content of our gratitude should be focused on the spiritual work He has done, is doing, and has yet to do in their lives.

Heavenly Father, thank You for each of my children. Thank You for all You have done, are doing, and will do in their lives.

Expectant

Paul was not only consistent in his prayers and constant in his gratitude—he was also confident in his expectation. He prayed believing that God was not finished yet. God still had more and better ahead. Let's look at several examples.

Now may the God of hope fill you with all joy and peace in believing, that you may abound in hope by the power of the Holy Spirit. Now I myself am confident concerning you, my brethren, that you also are full of goodness, filled with all knowledge, able also to admonish one another (Romans 15:13-14).

Notice that Paul bases his prayers on the confidence he has in them. Because God is in them, they have goodness, knowledge, and ability.

I thank my God always concerning you for the grace of God which was given to you by Christ Jesus, that you were enriched in everything by Him in all utterance and all knowledge, even as the testimony of Christ was confirmed in you, so that you come short in no gift, eagerly waiting for the revelation of our Lord Jesus Christ, who will also confirm you to the end, that you may be blameless in the day of our Lord Jesus Christ. God is faithful, by whom you were called into the fellowship of His Son, Jesus Christ our Lord (1 Corinthians 1:4-9).

Note that this is what he prays for the Corinthians, his most troublesome group of spiritual children. Yet, he was confident that one day even they would end up blameless because *God is faithful.* We can pray for our children with great expectation because we are praying to a great and faithful God.

I thank my God upon every remembrance of you, always in every prayer of mine making request for you all with joy, for your fellowship in the gospel from the first day until now, being confident of this very thing, that He who has begun a good work in you will complete it until the day of Jesus Christ (Philippians 1:3-6).

69

Note carefully the last verse. Paul says that he prays from a foundation of confidence that the same God who had begun a good work in them would complete it. Eugene Petersen renders this verse as, "*There has never been the slightest doubt in my mind that the God who started this great work in you would keep at it and bring it to a flourishing finish on the very day Christ Jesus appears.*" (Phil. 1:6 MSG). As we have said, there will be times when our children disappoint us. We must be like Paul and remember that our faith is not so much in them as in the God who is at work in them. As long as they are breathing, He is not finished working.

> *Now to Him who is able to do exceedingly abundantly above all that we ask or think, according to the power that works in us, to Him be glory in the church by Christ Jesus to all generations, forever and ever. Amen* (Ephesians 3:20-21).

Read those verses again, slowly. What an encouraging promise! We pour our hearts out to God on behalf of our children and it not only makes us feel better, it accomplishes something. God is able. He can do far more than we could ever imagine or guess or request in our wildest dreams. He is powerful. His power works in us and in our children so that it will all ultimately add up to His glory.

Too often the aim of our prayers is much too low. Paul prayed expectantly that his spiritual children would not just barely make God's team and ride the bench, but that they would hit spiritual homeruns and end up in the hall of faith. God is able and willing to work. He can do more than we can ask or imagine.

> *Mighty God, I praise You because Your dreams for my children are even bigger than my dreams for them. You are faithful and able to do more and better than I could ever ask or even imagine.*

Spiritually

Paul was not only *consistent* in his prayers, constant in his *gratitude*, and confident in his expectation, but he was also consumed with their *spiritual* progress. He prayed that they would know God and all God had available for them (see Eph. 1:17-19); that they would have inner strength and live open to Christ, experiencing the full dimensions of His love (see Eph. 3:14-20); that they would learn to live much and wisely, bear spiritual fruit (see Phil. 1:9-11).

Paul prayed that they would be in step with God's will and live well as they work for Him with glorious and joyful endurance (see Col. 1:9-12); that they'd overflow with love, strength, and purity (see 1 Thess. 3:11-13); and that God would make them holy and whole inside and out (see 1 Thess. 5:23-24).

Paul prayed that they would be fit for what God has called them to be and that God would energize their efforts (see 2 Thess. 1:11-12); that they would experience spiritual encouragement and empowerment in their words and works (see 2 Thess. 2:16-17); and that as they share their faith they would understand just how amazing it is (see Philem. 1:6).

Unlike most of our prayers that tend to be based on our children's physical needs, academic challenges, sporting competitions, financial situations, and so forth, Paul's prayers are consumed with the spiritual state of his spiritual children. I am sure that he did mention other areas of need on occasion, but what composed the vast majority of his requests was their spiritual condition.

Beyond that, he prayed that they would not remain at their current levels of spiritual maturity. Repeatedly, his prayers are entwined with requests for their ongoing spiritual development and progress. For example, he asked that they would be *"increasing in the knowledge of God"* (Col. 1:10); that they would *"increase and abound in love to one another and to all"* (1 Thess. 3:12); and told them that he prayed that their *"faith grows exceedingly, and the love of every one of you all abounds toward each other"* (2 Thess. 1:3).

As I read Paul's prayers, I came away with the strong sense that I needed to make some changes. The content of my prayers is often too temporal, too external, and too superficial. We need to learn from Paul to focus our prayers on what is most important, the spiritual development of our children.

> *Heavenly Father, please continue to complete the spiritual work You have started in my children's lives.*

A Summary of Paul's Requests

We are fortunate that Paul recorded so many of his prayer requests for his spiritual children. They show us that he prayed for every possible aspect of the relationship with God and their spiritual development. These requests are summarized for you. Read slowly through the following list of 26 requests and mark the ones you think are especially appropriate to pray for your children at this time.

Paul prayed that his spiritual children would...

Romans 15:5-6 *Learn to live in unity and harmony with others.*

Romans 15:13 *Be filled with joy, peace, and spiritual energy.*

Ephesians 1:17 *Know God personally.*

Ephesians 1:18 *Know what God is calling them to do and be, all that is available to them in God, and how great God's power can be in them as they believe in Him.*

Ephesians 3:16 *Be inwardly strengthened with Spirit-imparted power.*

Ephesians 3:17 *Have faith to be fully open to Christ and make Him welcome in their hearts.*

Ephesians 3:18 *Experience an ever-growing realization of every possible dimension of Christ's extravagant love.*

Ephesians 3:19 *Live full of God.*

Philippians 1:9 *Possess abounding, insightful, discerning, appropriate love.*

Philippians 1:10 *Wisely prioritize the best things.*

Philippians 1:10 *Be blamelessly pure.*

Philippians 1:11 *Be filled with righteous fruits.*

Colossians 1:9 *Be filled with a clear knowledge of God's will.*

Colossians 1:10 *Live worthy of the Lord consciously.*

Colossians 1:10 *Fully please Him in everything.*

Colossians 1:10 *Bear fruit in good works.*

Colossians 1:10 *Be filled with a clear knowledge of God.*

Colossians 1:11 *Be invigorated with glorious strength and endurance.*

Colossians 1:12 *Joyfully thank God for all He has made available to them.*

1 Thessalonians 3:12 *Abound in and overflow with love.*

1 Thessalonians 3:13 *Be infused with strength and blameless holiness.*

1 Thessalonians 5:23 *Be made holy and whole, inside and out.*

2 Thessalonians 1:11 *Be made fit for what God has called them to be.*

2 Thessalonians 1:11 *God would energize and fulfill their spiritual ideas and efforts.*

2 Thessalonians 2:17 *Experience spiritual encouragement and empowerment in their words and works.*

Philemon 1:6 *Share their faith and understand just how amazing it is.*

Putting It All Together

Take a few minutes and pray through the requests that grabbed your attention. As you do so, mark your prayers with gratitude for all God has already done, is currently doing, and will do for your children in the future. Pray expectantly that God will be bringing this request to pass. Also pray for wisdom as to how you can make this request a consistent part of your prayers for your children.

Lord, as I read these requests I am challenged to pray more consistently, more gratefully, more expectantly, and much more spiritually for my children. May they indeed experience all that You have for them in overflowing measure.

*You don't really understand human
nature unless you know why a child
on a merry-go-round will wave at his
parents every time around—and why
his parents will always wave back.*

—William D. Tammeus
(http://www.quotegarden.com/parents.html)

*I remember your genuine faith, for you share
the faith that first filled your grandmother Lois
and your mother, Eunice. And I know that same faith continues
strong in you* (2 Timothy 1:5 NLT).

*But you must remain faithful to the things you have been
taught. You know they are true, for you know you can trust
those who taught you. You have been taught the holy Scriptures
from childhood, and they have given you the wisdom to receive
the salvation that comes by trusting in Christ Jesus* (2 Timothy
3:14-15 NLT).

CHAPTER 5

Praying for Prodigals

We all know prodigals.

David Delk, president of Man in the Mirror Ministries, quotes statistics that 85 percent of children in America drop out of church before graduation; of those, only 40 percent return. Said another way, currently only 60 percent of children raised in church follow Jesus as adults.[1] That means 40 percent of the children in our churches this past Sunday will grow up to become spiritual prodigals.

We all have prodigals in our lives and in our families. Even Billy and Ruth Graham, the best-known Christians of this past century, saw two of their five children live as spiritual wanderers, going through ugly seasons of rebellion, drinking, and drug abuse before eventually returning to the Lord. Another of their children experienced the pain of two broken marriages and saw her children go through a painful series of out-of-wedlock pregnancies, drug use, and eating disorders.[2]

O Lord, give me hope for the prodigals in my family.
And Lord, not me only, but for all who
have a prodigal in their family, give hope.

We have found that it is possible to pray prodigals home. Whether it is a prodigal son or daughter, mother or father, sister or brother, husband or wife, it is possible to pray them home.

Luke's Gospel records what is easily the greatest father-son story ever told—Jesus' tale of the prodigal son and the loving father. First read through the whole story. Then we'll go back and take a practical look at it through the lens of parenthood and praying your prodigals home.

Then He said: "A certain man had two sons. And the younger of them said to his father, 'Father, give me the portion of goods that falls to me.' So he divided to them his livelihood. And not many days after, the younger son gathered all together, journeyed to a far country, and there wasted his possessions with prodigal living. But when he had spent all, there arose a severe famine in that land, and he began to be in want. Then he went and joined himself to a citizen of that country, and he sent him into his fields to feed swine. And he would gladly have filled his stomach with the pods that the swine ate, and no one gave him anything.

"But when he came to himself, he said, 'How many of my father's hired servants have bread enough and to spare, and I perish with hunger! I will arise and go to my father, and will say to him, "Father, I have sinned against heaven and before you, and

78

I am no longer worthy to be called your son. Make me like one of your hired servants.'"

"And he arose and came to his father. But when he was still a great way off, his father saw him and had compassion, and ran and fell on his neck and kissed him. And the son said to him, 'Father, I have sinned against heaven and in your sight, and am no longer worthy to be called your son.'

"But the father said to his servants, 'Bring out the best robe and put it on him, and put a ring on his hand and sandals on his feet. And bring the fatted calf here and kill it, and let us eat and be merry; for this my son was dead and is alive again; he was lost and is found.' And they began to be merry." (Luke 15:11-24).

Lessons From the Father

This story can be read on two levels. First, it is the story of a human father and a rebellious son. Second, it is the story of our heavenly Father and His children. In it we can see at least seven clear lessons we can learn from the father of the prodigal son.

1.   The father gave his son the opportunity to make mistakes.

It is hard to give someone rope when they have shown that they might just hang themselves with it. I (Dave) admire this father's willingness to let his son make mistakes.

2.   The father did not let his reputation keep him from doing what he thought was right.

The way the son left would have made the father a target for criticism and gossip in their community. If we are going to effectively minister to the prodigals in our families, we must not allow our reputation to get in the way.

3.   *The father refused to bail his son out of the mess he made.*

This is hard. We hate to see our kids suffer. But the father wisely understood that the pain of the mess is much less than the ultimate destruction brought on by an unchecked prodigal lifestyle.

4.   *The father did not give up hope.*

As long as your prodigal is breathing, there is hope. You may have looked hopeless at one time, but God has revolutionized your life.

5.   *The father kept the light on and the welcome mat out for the son to come home.*

A college friend of mine, Drew, had a dad who was the pastor of a large and influential church. In his teen years, Drew went through a rough period of rebellion. Of those years he writes,

> One of the most powerful memories I have of my prodigal years in high school is my Dad devotedly coming to my bedside at night to touch my arm, rub my forehead, and tell me he loved me. He knew my heart was far from him—and God. And he must have known that his expressions of love would not be reciprocated, but rejected. Still he came in, sat down on my bedside, and in effect hung a "Welcome Home" sign for me.[3]

6.   *The father extended full forgiveness.*

When the son returned, the father gave unconditional forgiveness! Forgiveness does not mean that you forget the pain and hurt. It does mean that you choose not to let it affect your treatment of the offender.

7. *The father probably had been praying all the time.*

It's not explicitly stated in the text, but the fact that the father saw his son coming a long way off tells me that he had been praying and believing all the time.

Strategies for Praying Prodigals Home

From this story, I find nearly a dozen insights into how to pray for prodigals.

1. *Ask the Father to parent the prodigal.*

Remind God that the prodigal is one of His own children—at least as the Creator. Ask Him to lovingly protect them, discipline them, and draw them to Himself. Ask the Lord to go rescue the prodigal as a shepherd rescues a lamb that strays from the flock.

2. *Pray that you don't get bitter.*

The father refused to get bitter. Parents who have had a child rebel against them and their values can experience intense pain and despair. When they see their own children walk away from all they want for them—and especially a relationship with God—it can be as upsetting as watching them die.

3. *Pray for the grace to let them go.*

The prodigal's father let his son go. He didn't lay a religious guilt trip on his son, but instead let him go. Pray for grace not to lay judgment on the prodigal. Pray for grace to keep your mouth shut and your heart open with love and compassion. Pray for grace not to speak critically or judgmentally.

4. Pray for endurance.

We don't know how long the prodigal was gone. The father had a huge estate and it would have taken years to blow through it. Plus, after the son spent all the money, he spent time feeding pigs. It can take years to see the fruit of intercession for prodigals. Keep praying.

5. Pray for famine.

But when he had spent all, there arose a severe famine in that land, and he began to be in want (Luke 15:14).

The boy ran out of money and got hungry more quickly because there was a famine in the land. Pray that whatever or whoever they are placing their trust in—outside of Jesus—would dry up. Pray for disillusionment toward the very things that once drew them and held them captive. Pray that what once brought them pleasure would be dry and barren to them. Pray that the novelty will wear off.

There was a time when one of my sons foolishly insisted on leaving home and doing his thing, his way. We prayed specifically that he would get cold and hungry, and would want to come home.

He did get cold and hungry.

Then he came home.

6. Pray for holy hunger or holy homesickness.

But when he came to himself, he said, "How many of my father's hired servants have bread enough and to spare, and I perish with hunger!" (Luke 15:17)

Pray that they'd get spiritually hungry and thirsty. Pray that they would long for the relationship they once had with their family, church, and the Father.

7.   Pray he or she would come to their senses.

"But when he came to himself." Pray the young person would realize something is wrong. Pray for their eyes to be opened to the truth of their situation, and pray against the delusion the enemy would try to bring.

8.   Pray for gifts of repentance.

"I will arise and go to my Father." Repentance describes a change of mind leading to a change of heart and then a resulting change of behavior. It means to turn and go in a new direction. Spiritual repentance is a spiritual gift. Ask the Father to give your prodigal the gift of repentance.

9.   Pray that the prodigal will have the ability to receive the grace of God.

Pray that the prodigal would be able to receive the Father's love and forgiveness. Some prodigals may have lived very immoral lives and they can't imagine the Father ever wanting them back. They feel as if they have crossed some sort of line so that the Lord would not be able to bless them again.

10. Pray for "welcoming love."

Pray for a love that would be open and warm to the prodigals even when they are still in sin. Love does not mean condoning their actions, but does mean wanting what is best for them, doing what is best for them. It is accepting them even when you cannot accept their behavior. Pray from the disposition of love, not of judgment and anger.

11. *Pray that the Lord will pour out His riches when the prodigal returns.*

Ask the Lord to lavish His love on the prodigal. Pray that when the prodigal returns that he or she will receive blessing upon blessing—spiritually, emotionally, mentally, physically, and financially.

It Works!

Some of you are saying, but I *have* prayed for the prodigals in my life. Let me encourage you—don't stop! It does work. Let me tell you my own prodigal story.

My sister Carol (who is 12 years older than I [Dave] am), was the number one girl in the youth group of our church. She went to college and fell in love with a young man named Don. Don was a Catholic and not yet born again. Carol asked our pastor at the time if they could be married in our home church; he refused. Our pastor said that joining Carol, a Baptist, with Don, a Catholic, would create an unequal yoke (see 2 Cor. 6:14). This made Carol bitter and she dropped out of church.

A few years later, the same pastor married his son, a Baptist, to a Catholic girl in our church. This made my mom bitter. She became a person who seemed to at best barely tolerate God. She only attended church on Sunday mornings, sat in the back, came late, and left early. I don't recall ever seeing her read her Bible during that time. I never heard her pray. She never spoke about spiritual things. In fact when I told her I thought God was calling me to be a pastor, her reply was, "Oh, no. Not that."

Concerned for my sister and my mother, I put both names on my daily prayer list. After years of daily calling Mom's name out to God, something happened. Cathy and I were meeting my parents at a restaurant when my mom walked in with a new countenance. The hard, heavy clouded-over expression was replaced with a bright sunny smile. During the meal, I was shocked to hear my ultra-quiet Mom speak with the waitress about her relationship with Christ. As we walked to the parking lot, my mother shocked me again by putting Gospel pamphlets on the windshields of the cars. She had turned into an evangelist!

"Mom," I asked, "What on earth has happened to you?"

She told us how she had been invited to a women's small group Bible study. There she learned to let go of her bitterness and yield everything to God. She also learned to pray for my sister. When Mom came home to God, Dad stepped up his relationship with God, too. Soon we were all praying regularly for Carol.

Things Got Worse

Have you ever prayed for something or someone and things got worse before they got better? That's what happened with my sister. We had prayed for her consistently for nearly a decade when one day, out of the blue, she called a family meeting. She and Don sat on one side of the table, Mom, Dad, Cathy, and I on the other.

"From now on," Carol said, "I do not want to be considered part of this family."

We were dumbfounded to hear my sister tell us she disowned us as her family.

The next thing we knew, she and Don got up and left. Very shortly after that, Carol left Don and moved to another state.

I have to admit that I quit praying for Carol because it did not seem to be working. Fortunately, Mom and Dad did not stop. Every day they called Carol's name out to God.

We did not see her or hear from her for years. One day our youngest son Luke was looking at an old family photo album. He pointed at a picture of a lady and asked, "Daddy who is that lady with you and Mommy?"

It was Carol. He could not remember ever seeing her before.

A Christmas Surprise

One Christmas Eve as I got up to lead one of several Christmas Eve services at our church, I looked out in the audience and was shocked by what I saw. About halfway back, on the middle aisle sat Carol, Don, and their two daughters. We spoke with them after the service and were surprised to find that they had recently gotten back together and had moved from a town 75 miles away to a town only 15 minutes away from our church.

Carol began to attend some of our family events and even came to our church about once a month. One Saturday while we watched my boys at a sporting event, she surprised me again.

"I think I would join your church," she stated, "except for three things."

After regaining my composure, I asked, "What are the three things?"

"I think abortion is all right; I think homosexuality is OK; and I hate Jerry Falwell."

I chuckled at her third excuse, but I could see that she was serious. "Well," I started, "you have been to our church enough times now to know that the big issue is Jesus Christ. What we focus on is a person's relationship with Jesus, not abortion, homosexuality, or Jerry Falwell. We believe that once you have a real relationship with Him, you can read the Bible and see what He thinks about abortion, homosexuality, or Jerry Falwell."

That seemed to satisfy her and she started coming to church every Sunday morning.

> ## "It's good to be home."

A few months later, I walked up on the platform to lead a Sunday evening celebration of the Lord's Table. When I looked out into the audience I was shocked to see my sister sitting about halfway back on the middle aisle. We had an amazing time with the Lord that night as we seriously considered His death, burial, and resurrection for our sins. We confessed our sins and praised His name.

After the service I was walking down the aisle to go into the lobby to meet people. Carol grabbed me as I approached her and put me in a bear hug. I noticed tears on her face as she leaned to whisper in my ear. I will never forget what she said.

"It's good to be home," she said. "It's been 30 years since I celebrated the Lord's Table and it is so good to finally be home."

The Rest of the Story

A few years later, Mom went to Heaven. The last few years of her life she had become a mighty prayer warrior. Less than five feet tall and weighing less than 100 pounds, she prayed with a simple, direct faith that got amazing results. Now she was gone. I remember bemoaning the fact that my best prayer partner was no longer with us. I wondered who would ever take her place.

About a week later we had a family get together at my sister's house. Exactly as my mom had done, she made us all grab hands and led us in a prayer. It was eerily familiar. She prayed with simple, direct faith exactly like Mom had done.

Beyond that, Carol has become quite a spiritual fireball in her own right. She has traveled the world on mission trips. She went from being in a small-group Bible study, to leading one, to now coaching 15 women's Bible study leaders.

I love to tell her story. It reminds us that it is possible to pray prodigal loved ones home.

The Rest of the Story...Part Two

I was speaking at a church one Friday night and I concluded the message by telling how prayer had brought Mom and Carol home to God. When I gave an opportunity for people to come and pray for prodigal loved ones, many responded. One couple especially caught my attention because they seemed especially broken as they wept at the prayer altar.

After the service they told me about their daughter Ashley. A 19-year-old, Ashley had run away from home six weeks earlier and they did not know where she was. We prayed a special prayer for God to touch Ashley's heart and call her home. I looked at my watch and prayed, "Lord, we do not know where Ashley is, but you do. Right now, at 8:33 P.M., we ask that you would speak to her heart. Make her hungry for home. Bring her to her senses and call her home to you."

They thanked me and said they would not be able to come back the next night because of a prior commitment, but that they would be back on Sunday. I forgot about it. God did not.

The next night as I was speaking, I noticed a young lady I had not seen there the night before. I did not think anymore about it.

After the service I was standing in the lobby and the young lady ran up to me and hugged me.

Taken aback by her forwardness I asked, "Who are you?"

"I'm Ashley," she said. "Last night at 8:33 I had an overwhelming longing to go home. I went home to Mom and Dad. Tonight I came home to God."

We all know prodigals. I hope the story of the prodigal son and the stories I have shared in this chapter encourage you to keep praying until your prodigals come home.

Your Turn

Identify the prodigals in your life. Who are they? Is it your son or daughter? Is it your grandson or granddaughter? Your brother or sister? Mom or Dad? Your husband or wife? Ex-husband or ex-wife? Write the name(s) here: _____
_____. Determine to pray for them until they come home to their heavenly Father.

> Determine to pray for your prodigals until they "come home" to their heavenly Father.

Lord, I pray for the prodigal(s) in my life.
Please parent them. Pursue them. Draw them to you.
Their rebellion against You has hurt us and others.
Please keep us from getting bitter toward them.
Help us persist in praying until they come home.
If necessary, dry up the relationships and circumstances
they are trusting in more than you.
Make them spiritually hungry and thirsty. Make them
homesick for us, for church, and for You.
Help them come to their senses.
Give them the gift to repent, to change directions, and
"come home" to You.
Help them receive Your grace. Pour out undeserved
blessing on them after they come back to You.

Endnotes

1. Patrick Morley and David Delk, "Father Five: Reversing the Generational Spiral," *A Look in the Mirror #108*, Man in the Mirror, http://www.maninthemirror.org/alm/alm108.htm, (accessed March 3, 2009).

2. See Ruth Bell Graham, *Prodigals and Those Who Love Them* (Grand Rapids, MI: Baker Books, 1999).

3. Quoted in Quin Sherrer and Ruthanne Garlock, *Praying Prodigals Home* (Ventura, CA: Regal Books, 2000), 197-198.

Don't worry that children never listen to you; worry that they are always watching you.

—Robert Fulghum
(http://www.quotegarden.com/parents.html)

Had I Been Joseph's Mother

*Had I been Joseph's mother I'd have
prayed protection from his brothers, "God,
keep him safe. He is so young, so different
from the others." Mercifully, she never knew
there would be slavery and prison, too...*

*Had I been Daniel's mother I should have
pled, "Give victory!—this Babylonian horde
godless and cruel—Don't let him be a
captive—better dead, Almighty Lord!"*

*Had I been Mary, Oh, had I been she,
I would have cried as never a mother cried, "Anything, O God,
Anything...—but crucified."*

*With such prayers importunate my finite
wisdom would assail Infinite Wisdom. God,
how fortunate Infinite Wisdom should prevail.*

—Ruth Bell Graham, *Prodigals
and Those Who Love Them*

CHAPTER 6

How to Pray for Children Seven Days a Week

O Lord, give me a daily burden for my children.
Teach me how to pray for them, and
lead me into effective intercession.

As parents, we are careful to meet the physical, material, and emotional needs of our children every day. We should be just as careful to pray for them and their spiritual needs daily. In this chapter, I (Dave) want to encourage you to pray for your children every day, and to make sure that at least part of your prayers are for their spiritual needs.

As previously noted, Paul repeatedly mentioned the constancy and consistency of his prayers for his spiritual children. He prayed for them gratefully, expectantly, and spiritually. I find that as a parent I often do well remembering their pressing physical, material, vocational, or academic needs in prayer. But it can be easy to miss their spiritual needs, which truly are the most important.

I have found that it is easier for me to stay consistent on praying for my children's spiritual needs when I use some sort of simple system. Over the years, I find that I tend to use one of these two systems.

Praying Daily

Children go through various and challenging seasons in their spiritual journeys. Often God places a specific Scripture on my heart that seems to wonderfully fit the season one of my children is facing.

I am a person who practices the spiritual discipline of journaling. While the front of my journal is used as a diary, the back of my journal contains my prayer lists. I go through a journal about every three months. So every three months when I start a new journal, I recreate my prayer lists in the back of the journal. One of the lists is for my immediate family members. On that list, I usually select a scriptural prayer that I want to pray for them each day.

About a year ago, all of our three sons seemed to be wrestling with three primary issues: an unusual level of spiritual attack, a need to kick it up a gear in their spiritual lives, and they were struggling to discover God's calling in their lives. As I considered several possible scriptural prayers I could pray for them, I settled on the prayer Jesus offered His disciples as recorded in John 17. Note how well it addresses the same three needs my sons were facing.

My prayer is not that you take them out of the world but that you protect them from the evil one. They are not of the world, even as I am not of it. Sanctify them by the truth; your word is truth. As you sent me into the world, I have sent them into the world (John 17:15-18 NIV).

Taking this passage as the foundation, I made these requests my requests. So every day, I prayed this John 17 prayer of Jesus that the Lord would:

1. **Protect them from the evil one.**

2. **Sanctify them through the truth of His Word.**

3. **Clarify their calling as sent into the world.**

There were a few bumps in the road, but by the end of the several months of praying the John 17 prayer daily, the results were amazing. All three had come victoriously through their season of spiritual attack and seemed to be entering a season of rest, stability, and progress. All three also took noticeable steps of spiritual growth and sanctification as they placed themselves in settings where they were exposed more frequently to the Word of God. Also, all three got involved in weekly ministries.

Beyond that, our eldest son changed his major in college to Biblical Studies so he could pursue becoming a senior pastor. My middle son also surrendered to the call to vocational church ministry and changed his major so he could pursue his calling as a children's pastor. Our youngest son selected English as his major as he felt God was directing him to become an editor and/or author.

I usually pray the same passage daily until one of three things occurs. First, God answers. Second, the burden corresponding to one Scripture is replaced by a burden related to another.

Third, I start a new journal and decide that it is time to pray another passage.

At the end of this chapter you will find a list of other scriptural prayers you can use for praying for your loved ones. You may want to pick one that seems to fit the needs of your family and pray it every day until it becomes a reality.

> **Pray a different Scripture for your children for each day of the week.**

Praying Weekly

There are times when they may have needs that are not expressed by one passage. There are also other times when there are no pressing spiritual needs. In order to be proactive, pray for them regarding their entire spiritual experience. During these times, I suggest selecting seven passages of Scripture that address a variety of spiritual areas and pray a different one each day of the week. It might look like this:

Monday

Dear friend, I pray that you may enjoy good health and that all may go well with you, even as your soul is getting along well. It gave me great joy to have some brothers come and tell about your faithfulness to the truth and how you continue to walk in the truth. I have no greater joy than to hear that my children are walking in the truth (3 John 1:2-4 NIV).

96

1. **Good health.**

2. **Spiritual progress and prosperity.**

3. **Walk in the truth.**

Tuesday

Simon, Simon, Satan has asked to sift you as wheat. But I have prayed for you, Simon, that your faith may not fail. And when you have turned back, strengthen your brothers (Luke 22:31-32 NIV).

1. **Unfailing faith.**

2. **Use all their mistakes to ultimately help others.**

Wednesday

Now may our God and Father himself and our Lord Jesus clear the way for us to come to you. May the Lord make your love increase and overflow for each other and for everyone else, just as ours does for you. May He strengthen your hearts so that you will be blameless and holy in the presence of our God and Father when our Lord Jesus comes with all His holy ones (1 Thessalonians 3:11-13 NIV).

1. **Increasing, overflowing love.**

2. **Strengthened hearts.**

3. **Blameless holiness.**

Thursday

And this is my prayer: that your love may abound more and more in knowledge and depth of insight, so that you may be able to discern what is best and may be pure and blameless until the day of Christ, filled with the fruit of righteousness that comes through Jesus Christ—to the glory and praise of God (Philippians 1:9-11).

1. **Abounding, accurate, and appropriate love.**

2. **Discern the best over the good.**

3. **Blameless purity.**

4. **Righteous fruit.**

Friday

I keep asking that the God of our Lord Jesus Christ, the glorious Father, may give you the Spirit of wisdom and revelation, so that you may know him better. I pray also that the eyes of your heart may be enlightened in order that you may know the hope to which he has called you, the riches of his glorious inheritance in the saints, and his incomparably great power for us who believe... (Ephesians 1:17-19 NIV).

1. **Know and experience God deeply and progressively.**

2. **Know and experience all God has for them in terms of hope, calling, and lifestyle.**

Saturday

For this reason, since the day we heard about you, we have not stopped praying for you and asking God to fill you with the knowledge of his will through all spiritual wisdom and understanding. And we pray this in order that you may live a life worthy of the Lord and may please him in every way: bearing fruit in every good work, growing in the knowledge of God, being strengthened with all power according to his glorious might so that you may have great endurance and patience, and joyfully giving thanks to the Father, who has qualified you to share in the inheritance of the saints in the kingdom of light (Colossians 1:9-12 NIV).

1. **Know God's will.**

2. **Live worthy of and pleasing to God.**

3. **Bear spiritual fruit.**

4. **Grow in their knowledge of God.**

5. **Grow in spiritual strength and endurance.**

6. **Live a life of gratitude.**

Sunday

With this in mind, we constantly pray for you, that our God may count you worthy of his calling, and that by his power he may fulfill every good purpose of yours and every act prompted by your faith. We pray this so that the name of our Lord Jesus may be glorified in you, and you in him, according to the grace of our God and the Lord Jesus Christ (2 Thessalonians 1:11-12).

1. **Be made fit for what God has called them to be.**

2. **God would energize and fulfill their spiritual ideas and efforts.**

3. **Jesus would be glorified in them.**

> **Pray a different passage each day of the month.**

Praying Monthly

Recorded in the Bible are a month's worth of blessings and prayers that we could pray for each other. You may want to pray one each day as you go through the month. When you are finished, you can start over. If you miss a day, simply pick up where you left off. This way you will be covering every aspect of your children's spiritual progress by praying scriptural prayers each day.

Numbers 6:24-26 NIV

The Lord bless you and keep you; the Lord make his face shine upon you and be gracious to you; the Lord turn his face toward you and give you peace.

1 Chronicles 22:11-13

Now, my son, may the Lord be with you; and may you prosper, and build the house of the Lord your God, as He has said to you. Only may the Lord give you wisdom and understanding, and give you charge concerning Israel, that you may keep the law of the Lord your God. Then you will prosper, if you take care to fulfill the statutes and judgments with which the Lord charged Moses concerning Israel. Be strong and of good courage; do not fear nor be dismayed."

Psalm 20:1-4

May the Lord answer you in the day of trouble; May the name of the God of Jacob defend you; may He send you help from the sanctuary, and strengthen you out of Zion; may He remember all your offerings, and accept your burnt sacrifice. Selah. May He grant you according to your heart's desire, and fulfill all your purpose.

Psalm 67:1-2 (NIV)

May God be gracious to us and bless us and make his face shine upon us, Selah, that your ways may be known on earth, your salvation among all nations.

Luke 22:31-32 (NIV)

Simon, Simon, Satan has asked to sift you as wheat. But I have prayed for you, Simon, that your faith may not fail. And when you have turned back, strengthen your brothers.

John 17:15-18 (NIV)

My prayer is not that you take them out of the world but that you protect them from the evil one. They are not of the world, even as I am not of it. Sanctify them by the truth; your word is truth. As you sent me into the world, I have sent them into the world.

Romans 1:8-12 (NIV)

First, I thank my God through Jesus Christ for all of you, because your faith is being reported all over the world. God, whom I serve with my whole heart in preaching the gospel of his Son, is my witness how constantly I remember you in my prayers at all times; and I pray that now at last by God's will the way may be opened for me to come to you. I long to see you so that I may impart to you some spiritual gift to make you strong—that is, that you and I may be mutually encouraged by each other's faith.

Romans 15:5-6

Now may the God of patience and comfort grant you to be likeminded toward one another, according to Christ Jesus, that you may with one mind and one mouth glorify the God and Father of our Lord Jesus Christ.

Romans 15:13

Now may the God of hope fill you with all joy and peace in believing, that you may abound in hope by the power of the Holy Spirit.

Romans 15:33

Now the God of peace be with you all. Amen.

1 Corinthians 1:4-9 (NIV)

I always thank God for you because of His grace given you in Christ Jesus. For in Him you have been enriched in every way— in all your speaking and in all your knowledge—because our testimony about Christ was confirmed in you. Therefore you do not lack any spiritual gift as you eagerly wait for our Lord Jesus Christ to be revealed. He will keep you strong to the end, so that you will be blameless on the day of our Lord Jesus Christ. God, who has called you into fellowship with His Son Jesus Christ our Lord, is faithful.

2 Corinthians 13:14 (NIV)

May the grace of the Lord Jesus Christ, and the love of God, and the fellowship of the Holy Spirit be with you all.

Galatians 6:18 (NIV)

The grace of our Lord Jesus Christ be with your spirit, brothers. Amen.

Ephesians 1:17-19 (NIV)

I keep asking that the God of our Lord Jesus Christ, the glorious Father, may give you the Spirit of wisdom and revelation, so that you may know Him better. I pray also that the eyes of your heart may be enlightened in order that you may know the hope to which He has called you, the riches of His glorious inheritance in the saints, and His incomparably great power for us who believe....

Ephesians 3:14-19 (NIV)

For this reason I kneel before the Father, from whom his whole family in heaven and on earth derives its name. I pray that out of His glorious riches he may strengthen you with power through his Spirit in your inner being, so that Christ may dwell in your hearts through faith. And I pray that you, being rooted and established in love, may have power, together with all the saints, to grasp how wide and long and high and deep is the love of Christ, and to know this love that surpasses knowledge—that you may be filled to the measure of all the fullness of God.

Ephesians 6:23-24 (NIV)

Peace to the brothers, and love with faith from God the Father and the Lord Jesus Christ. Grace to all who love our Lord Jesus Christ with an undying love.

Philippians 1:3-6 (NIV)

I thank my God every time I remember you. In all my prayers for all of you, I always pray with joy because of your partnership in the gospel from the first day until now, being confident of this, that he who began a good work in you will carry it on to completion until the day of Christ Jesus.

Philippians 4:23 (NIV)

The grace of the Lord Jesus Christ be with your spirit. Amen.

Colossians 1:3-6 (NIV)

We always thank God, the Father of our Lord Jesus Christ, when we pray for you, because we have heard of your faith in Christ Jesus and of the love you have for all the saints—the faith and love that spring from the hope that is stored up for you in heaven and that you have already heard about in the word of truth, the gospel that has come to you....

Colossians 1:9-12 (NIV)

For this reason, since the day we heard about you, we have not stopped praying for you and asking God to fill you with the knowledge of His will through all spiritual wisdom and understanding. And we pray this in order that you may live a life worthy of the Lord and may please Him in every way: bearing fruit in every good work, growing in the knowledge of God, being strengthened with all power according to His glorious might so that you may have great endurance and patience, and joyfully giving thanks to the Father, who has qualified you to share in the inheritance of the saints in the kingdom of light.

1 Thessalonians 1:2-3 (NIV)

We always thank God for all of you, mentioning you in our prayers. We continually remember before our God and Father your work produced by faith, your labor prompted by love, and your endurance inspired by hope in our Lord Jesus Christ.

1 Thessalonians 2:13 (NIV)

And we also thank God continually because, when you received the word of God, which you heard from us, you accepted it not as the word of men, but as it actually is, the word of God, which is at work in you who believe.

1 Thessalonians 5:23-24 (NIV)

May God Himself, the God of peace, sanctify you through and through. May your whole spirit, soul and body be kept blameless at the coming of our Lord Jesus Christ. The One who calls you is faithful and He will do it.

2 Thessalonians 1:3-4 (NIV)

We ought always to thank God for you, brothers, and rightly so, because your faith is growing more and more, and the love every one of you has for each other is increasing. Therefore, among God's churches we boast about your perseverance and faith in all the persecutions and trials you are enduring.

2 Thessalonians 1:11-12 (NIV)

With this in mind, we constantly pray for you, that our God may count you worthy of His calling, and that by His power He may fulfill every good purpose of yours and every act prompted by your faith. We pray this so that the name of our Lord Jesus may be glorified in you, and you in Him, according to the grace of our God and the Lord Jesus Christ.

2 Thessalonians 3:5 (NIV)

May the Lord direct your hearts into God's love and Christ's perseverance.

2 Thessalonians 3:16 (NIV)

Now may the Lord of peace Himself give you peace at all times and in every way. The Lord be with all of you.

Philemon 1:4-6 (NIV)

I always thank my God as I remember you in my prayers, because I hear about your faith in the Lord Jesus and your love for all the saints. I pray that you may be active in sharing your faith, so that you will have a full understanding of every good thing we have in Christ.

Hebrews 13:20-21 (NIV)

May the God of peace, who through the blood of the eternal covenant brought back from the dead our Lord Jesus, that great Shepherd of the sheep, equip you with everything good for doing His will, and may He work in us what is pleasing to Him, through Jesus Christ, to whom be glory for ever and ever. Amen.

Don't Forget...

As you consider how the Lord would like you to pray scriptural prayers for your children, be reminded of two very encouraging truths. First, as we are faithful in praying, God is faithful in working. As Paul reminded the Corinthians, *"God, who has called you into fellowship with his Son Jesus Christ our Lord, is faithful"* (1 Cor. 1:9). Second, God is able to do more than we have asked for, or have even imagined. Remember the promise Paul gave the Ephesians:

> *Now to him who is able to do immeasurably more than all we ask or imagine, according to his power that is at work within us, to him be glory in the church and in Christ Jesus through-out all generations, forever and ever! Amen* (Ephesians 3:20-21 NIV).

Read the words of verse 21 again slowly— *"to him be glory in the church and in Christ Jesus throughout all generations, forever and ever!"* Remember, the ultimate point of all of our prayers for our children is that Jesus will receive such awesome glory through their lives that it will span generations.

Lord, Help me be constant and consistent in praying for the spiritual progress of my children. Lead me to the plan that will work best for us, and help me stick to it.

Always kiss your children goodnight—even if they're already asleep.

—Jackson Brown Jr.

(http://www.quotegarden.com/parents.html)

*The love of a mother is never exhausted. It never changes—it
never tires—it endures through all;
in good repute, in bad repute, in the face of the
world's condemnation, a mother's love still lives on.*

—Washington Irving
(http://www.familyofdestiny.com/article_16rules.htm)

CHAPTER 7

Preparing to Pray With Children

*Lord, the most important thing I ever do
with my children is to pray with them.
Teach me to do it as effectively as I can.*

Parents have a duty not only to pray *for* their children, but to
pray *with* their children. They cannot excuse themselves from
their responsibility, thinking that a pastor or Sunday school
teacher will pray for their children. Also, they should not trust
only in the prayers of grandparents, uncles, or aunts.

Perhaps the most powerful influence on your children's life
is when you lead them into the presence of God. This happens
when you kneel with them by the bed, bow your head, and fold

your hands as you all gather around the dinner table, or other times when you pray.

Since you come to God with your needs, isn't it understandable that your children should come to God with their needs? And, the time to teach your children to pray is when they first understand the words you speak to them. Let them see you pray for them even before they can or know how to pray. They will feel your concern for them because of your bowed head and folded hands, even before they understand what you are doing. Remember, you communicate your attitude to your children earlier than you communicate word-meanings or even prayer practices.

Lord, may I communicate my love for You
to my children and may my children imitate
the same love and faith I have in God.

1. You must take responsibility for their prayer support.

No one will pray for your children as effectively as you. Because God has given them to you, and because you gave birth to them, you are the ideal person to pray for them with love, conviction, and deep passion for God. You want God to protect and teach them, just as you do these things for them.

No one is better equipped to introduce children to God's love than their parents. And no one will pray as fervently for your children to be kept from temptation and the evil one than you.

And another thing, no one will invest as much time in your children in clothing, feeding, directing, and playing with them. You will do more to shape your children's values, because you become their first role model.

112

And their relationship to you as the authority will ultimately shape their relationship to God as their ultimate authority. Father, you will role model the children's relationship with their heavenly Father (see Luke 11:11-13). And Mother, you will role model love, wisdom, and patience like no other.

Pray with them and for them, especially after correcting your children for something they've done wrong. This is a great time to communicate forgiveness when you tell God that you forgive them, and then you pray with them for God's forgiveness. The time invested in praying for God's blessing on your children will return great results in their lives.

When children are young, we listen to them as they say their prayers. But also while they are young, they listen to us as we pray. When they get older, they will be praying for us while we listen to them.

2. *Parents must bring children to Jesus.*

You are the adult, so you must appoint the time and place. Then you must create the proper atmosphere where they pray (reverence), and then you must lead them in prayer. Jesus said, "Let the little children come to Me..." (Matt. 19:14 NIV). So, when you bring your children to God in prayer, you are obeying the exhortation of Jesus.

3. *Parents must not omit their responsibility to pray.*

God expects His children to come to Him in prayer, so when you lead your children to pray, you are bringing God's children into His presence. *"But the mercy of the Lord is from everlasting to everlasting on those who fear Him, and His righteousness to children's children, to such as keep His covenant, and to those who remember His commandments to do them"* (Ps. 103:17-18). This verse reminds us to keep the commandments of Christ and not omit praying for our children from our daily routine. We receive the mercy of the Lord when we bring our children to Him in prayer.

4. Ask yourself the question, "Can God trust me with my children?"

God gives us children as a stewardship. That means God trusts us with caring for His children. We must lead them to Christ, train them, teach them Christian character and Bible content, then provide opportunities for them to serve God all their lives. In a broad sense, God trusts the eternal destiny of children to us, their parents—as the parents live, so the children believe.

Abraham was a good parent, so much so that God trusted him with children. God said of Abraham, *"I have known him...that he may command his children and his household after him, that they keep the way of the Lord, to do righteousness and justice..."* (Gen. 18:19). So ask yourself the question, "Can God trust me to develop the prayer life of my children?"

*Lord, I want to develop my children
in the wonderful practices of prayer.*

5. Parents can teach prayer in natural, informal ways.

You don't need a formal classroom setting to teach prayer. You don't need to have a curriculum or textbook (the Bible is your textbook). You teach children how to pray as you informally walk through the daily issues of life. As you begin or finish the meal, teach your children to pray. As they're preparing for bed, teach your children to pray. As they leave the house to go to school, teach your children to pray.

Moses told us to teach our children as we sit in our house, as we walk by the road, as we lay down at night, and as we get up in

114

the morning (see Deut. 6:7). That sounds like Moses expected us to do it in informal ways.

Lord, help me to teach my children to pray at
every available time, in many informal
ways, with all the resources available to me.

6. Teach them to be a friend of God and that prayer is talking to God.

In the Old Testament, God called Abraham his friend (see Isa. 41:8), but in the New Testament Jesus said, *"You are my friends"* (John 15:14). And what do friends do? They chat, discuss, listen, and enjoy one another's company. So develop a friendship attitude between God and your children.

Explain to your children that prayer is our way of talking with the heavenly Father, and He hears what they are saying, and will answer them.

Make sure you tell your children that prayer is not a speech to God. They don't have to use grown-up words, nor do they have to use words like, "deity," "holy," or "reverence." Let them pray honestly from the heart, using their vocabulary.

Again, don't force your children to pray from your perspective because they don't live in your world, nor do they understand your needs. Allow a child to say, "Thank you for my new video game," or "Thank you for my new doll," or "I hurt my ankle, help me get well."

Make sure your children understand that God loves them and wants them to talk with Him in their language, from the needs of their world.

*Lord, I am a parent who is trying to
teach my children how to pray. Help me.*

7. Let your children learn to pray from your example.

You may not be a great prayer warrior, that's all right. Begin where you are, "Lord, I am a parent who is trying to teach my children how to approach You." Begin with, "Lord, I need to be an example to my children in prayer, so help me be a good role model."

Sometimes you might not even know the first thing to communicate to your children about prayer, so begin with the premise, "I must want them to learn how to pray." So you must learn to pray before you can teach them to pray, "Lord, I want my children to learn how to talk to You, so teach me how to talk to You; teach us (my children and me) how to be better friends with You."

Your children will learn by example, first from what they see (your reverence—kneeling, bowing, etc.) and second from what they hear (you must pray first). Make sure that the children see that you bring yourself before the Lord with a humble attitude, seeking things in your life that conform to His will.

Don't just pray for the needs of children when you kneel to pray with them. Pray for your own needs, too, so that your children know that you are just as needy as they are. As a father, pray about being a better person at work, or ask God to help you with a problem on the job. As a mother, pray that God would help you manage the house and raise the children. If you're a mother who also works outside the home, ask for patience and discipline to get both your day job and home job done in accordance with His will. When you pray sincerely, eventually you'll have your children praying for you. It is wonderful when they want to pray for you as you pray for them.

*Your children need your
presence more than your presents.*

—Jesse Jackson
(http://www.quotegarden.com/parents.html)

A Mother's Influence

*I took a piece of plastic clay and idly
fashioned it one day; and as my fingers
pressed it still it moved and yielded at my will.*

*I came again when days were past, the form
I gave it still it bore, and as my fingers
pressed it still, I could change that form no more.*

*I took a piece of living clay, and gently formed
it day by day, and molded with my power and
art, a young child's soft and yielding heart.*

*I came again when days were gone; it
was a man I looked upon, he still that early
impress bore, and I could change it never more.*

—Author Unknown

CHAPTER 8

Preparing Children to Pray

*Lord, I want my children to talk with You about
everything in their lives. I yield myself to Your instruction.
Teach me how to teach my children to pray.*

In the previous chapter we discussed how you get yourself
ready to pray. Now, even before you begin to teach your children
to pray, notice some of the things you must do to prepare them
to learn to pray.

1. Point out small blessings and answers to prayer.

Before you discuss prayer requests with your children, begin
by pointing out some of the things that God has helped them do
earlier that day. It could be as simple as the children learning a

task such as stacking dishes in the dishwasher, taking out the trash, or walking the dog.

Find out what the children have enjoyed that day by asking: "What was the most fun thing you did today?" As they tell you, remind them of God's blessing to give them joy and happiness. Even the smallest happiness should be pointed out whether it's a popsicle, a favorite television program, or a new video game. Remind the children that they must "thank God for the good times you had today." You want your children to get into the habit of thanking God for everything in their life that is enjoyable.

Lord, when unexpected things make me say, "WOW,"
remind me to pass my excitement on to my children.

2. Watch for the "WOW" times in life.

There are some things that grab our attention and make us yell, "WOW!" Talk about these with your children and pray with them about them. These may include an unexpected goal in soccer, a perfect paper in school, or other things that makes the kids open their eyes and giggle uncontrollably. Remind them to thank God for the small enjoyable things of life, as well as praise God for the "WOWs" in life.

Lord, You are a great teacher and
You created a great universe.

3. Teach your children to thank God for creation and the Creator.

From the very beginning, teach your children to enjoy creation as God has given it. Start with the different seasons of the year—summer, fall, winter, and spring. Each of these seasons brings special blessings and requires different attitudes from us. You might thank God for April showers, as well as thank Him for winter's snow. Thank God for a warm spring day to play outside, and thank God for the hot sun that makes crops grow to provide food for your children.

Next, point out the things they might see in nature on the way to school, whether it's a flowering bush, the autumn leaves on the sidewalk, or the man next door cutting his grass. Remind them that just as everything in nature grows, they too grow.

And when you think of nature, don't forget their dog, cat, and if not theirs, perhaps their grandparents or neighbors have an animal they enjoy. Again, remind them as their pets grow and learn, so they too should grow and learn. Tie all creation back to the Creator, teach your kids the attitude of gratitude. Make them thankful to God for everything in life that grows.

4. *Pray with them about unpleasant situations.*

All children will have stressful or unpleasant situations in school. This could be a bully who taunts them or someone who embarrasses them, or they could be shunned by those who were previous friends. Every school experience will have some hurts because that's the nature of the world in which they live.

Every parent would like to shield their children from the unpleasant situations of life. You can't do it, neither can anyone else. So we must teach our children: (a) unpleasantries will come, (b) they must adapt and adjust to unpleasant situations, and (c) they can learn to triumph over these situations and learn from them.

As you kneel by their bed at night, this can be a good time to talk about unpleasant situations and how they can cope with them through prayer.

Unpleasant situations may happen to others, such as passing an automobile accident, or hearing about a family who was murdered, or hearing about an airplane crash. Pray about these times as well.

Unpleasantness also happens within their extended family. This could be an aunt struggling with cancer, the death of a grandparent, or a friend's parents going through divorce, job loss, or other problems. During prayer time, call attention to the problem, and both you and your children pray to God for His perfect answer.

> *Lord, may my prayers to You be so natural that
> my children will naturally follow my example.*

5. Remember that prayer is better caught, than taught.

Sometimes it is difficult to explain some situations to children; in these cases, just you should pray about them. Let the child enter into your feelings, and let them agree with you in prayer, so they can adjust to situations; but at the same time are also learning that they should pray about them as well.

Show your children what it's like to pray on a regular basis for the problems and challenges of life. If you are deeply impressed that prayer makes a difference, your children will catch your attitude. If you naturally pray and bring these issues to the heavenly Father, your children will follow your example. If you have faith that the Father will work through these situations to His glory, again your children naturally develop the same strong faith in God.

*Don't handicap your children
by making their lives easy.*

—Robert A. Heinlein

(http://www.quotegarden.com/parents.html)

What a mother sings to the cradle
goes all the way down to the coffin.

—Henry Ward Beecher (1813–1887)

(http://en.proverbia.net/citastema.asp?tematica=630)

CHAPTER 9

Teaching Children to Pray

*Lord, I wait for the opportunity to hear a child
pray the first time. May I have the simple
faith to talk to You, as a little child.*

1. Always remember the real reason to pray.

Many children think they should pray to "get stuff" from God. They treat God like a spiritual Santa Clause. They bring a list of things to God that they want to receive. While praying for things is acceptable, there is something greater. That something greater is God Himself. Ask, "What does God get out of your children's prayers?" The only enduring motive for prayer is God Himself.

Every child has some sense of God's unseen presence in their lives. Validate this sense of God by teaching them to pray to their heavenly Father whenever the need arises.

First, teach them to pray in the privacy of their own heart when things happen. Remind them that there will be unpleasant days and embarrassing times. Encourage them to pray immediately rather than wait to pray with you at night.

Teach them to pray for the people involved and to pray for God's glory when they see an accident or other needs in life.

Teach them to practice the presence of God in their lives. Sometimes when they are older and driving to school, encourage them to communicate to God in prayer about the coming day, classes, and problems.

Teach them to pray when they are in bed at night before they go to sleep. When I (Elmer) can't go to sleep, I pray the Lord's Prayer, applying each of the petitions to my own personal life. This is not a rote-like repetition but praying its meaning in my life. (See Appendix A.)

> *Lord, I confess I'm often self-centered when I approach*
> *prayer. Forgive me for treating You as a Dispenser*
> *of Things. Teach me to come to You for Who You*
> *are, and to share this attitude with my children.*

2. **When you pray first, you teach by example.**

When your children are new at praying, it probably is a good idea for you to pray first. You might do it for the first few days when you are teaching them to pray. You might talk to God first before asking them to pray. You could begin with, "Do you want Mother/Father to pray about this?" or you might introduce it by saying, "Do you want me to talk to God about this before you pray?"

If a child is reluctant to pray the first few times you ask, that's OK. Just make sure they understand what you pray, and make sure they understand that prayer is a "friendship" relationship with the heavenly Father. Anyone can talk with a friend. Be careful not to use "ecclesiastical" words in your prayers so that you scare or confuse the children. Remember, children are not good at making speeches; but they're good at chatting with friends.

Lord, sometimes I have to think about the things I'm going to pray about before I pray. Have patience with me.

3.   Talk about suggested prayer topics before you talk to God.

What you don't want to do is ask for "prayer requests." You might do that in a prayer meeting, or even in an older group of adults, but children don't understand "prayer requests" until you've used that term many times. Rather, talk to your children about the things that the two of you will pray about. "What do you want to pray about tonight?" or "What do you want to thank God for today?" or "If you're going to thank God for the best thing that happened all day, what is it?"

If you're praying with more than one child, you might assign different topics to different children. You may want to say to the youngest one, "Why don't you pray for grandmother," or you may say to an older child, "Why don't you pray for the healing of Aunt Mary who is struggling with cancer."

When you ask children to pray about things, you're making them become sensitive to other people, and facing the needs of other people, and becoming concerned about other people. Isn't that another way of teaching them to love other people?

Lord, we all have bad days; help me (and my children)
take them in stride, just as I take prayer in stride.

4. **If your children have had a bad day, talk to God about it first,**
   so their heart is right before they pray about other things.

Start with the assumption that bad days either come from or result in bad attitudes such as anger, jealousy, spitefulness, or moodiness.

Early on you'll have to teach your children to deal with a bad attitude because they are angry, discouraged, or hurt. Have them say a very simple prayer such as, "God, forgive me for getting mad at..." Don't make it a big repentant speech, but sometimes you should expect tears or deep-seated repentance. Let children express their emotions at their own level.

When you are dealing with a bad day, remind the children. *"If we confess our sins, He is faithful and just to forgive us..."* (1 John 1:9). God will not only forgive, but He will cleanse and forget, *"The blood of Jesus Christ His son cleanses us from all sin"* (1 John 1:7).

When your children are angry or upset because things didn't go their way, remember there is an enemy who seeks to destroy your child (see 1 Pet. 5:8), and the devil will throw fiery darts at them to tempt them to sin (see Eph. 6:13).

5. **Teach honesty about their emotions.**

If they have had a tough day, ask God to help them get through it or change their attitude. Ask, "What good thing happened today?" Then "Let's thank God for it." Talk to them about being sad, angry, and guilty because of what they didn't do. It's important for them to talk about their feelings. Then let them know God is concerned about their feelings and that they should bring their emotions to God in prayer.

Lord, I love the spontaneous nature of children. Help me to be more spontaneous to You in my prayers.

6.   As you are discussing your prayer topics, expect diversions.

Your child may say, "I've got to go to the bathroom," or "Can I have a glass of water?" or "Are you going to drive me to school tomorrow?"

Long ago I (Elmer) learned that children have a very short attention span. The younger the child, the shorter the attention span; as they grow older, they can pay attention longer. So what does that mean? You should not expect them to pay attention for long periods of time.

I remember telling a story in children's church years ago, and I thought I had the children spellbound in rapt attention. One little girl glanced out the window, saw a blue bird, and quickly darted over to the window pointing and yelling, "Look at the blue bird." Immediately, all the eyes of the children went to the window, along with three or four pairs of feet. My story was crushed.

What did I do? I prayed, "God, help me." And He gave me a brilliant idea. I announced, "Let's all go to the window and see the blue bird." We went and I pointed out his beautiful feathers. Then suddenly, it flew away and I announced to the children, "There was a blue bird in the life of...." I forget who the Bible character was, but I described a blue bird in his life, got their attention and finished telling my story at the window where they were standing.

I know that most parents want to instruct their children in the deep things of faith, or challenge them to total dedication to God. But children can't respond as adults—children are children. As a matter of fact, one of the good things about having them close their eyes when praying is so they are not distracted with the world around them. That leads us to the next topic.

Lord, when we fold our hands, look
beyond our outward expression. Look into
our hearts, for we also fold it to You.

7. *Teach your children to fold their hands and close their eyes.*

The easiest way to get your children to fold their hands is for you to do it. If you get them to intertwine their little fingers, they are more likely to hold their hands together and that keeps little hands from straying, scratching, and reaching. If you put two little hands flat together, they will end up rubbing one hand with another, and before you know it, they are rubbing other parts of the body. So try to entwine their fingers and you'll find it's easier to get them to pray.

I have heard it said that a mother can fold a small baby's hands in her hands, and together they can reach all the way to Heaven. Even when a little baby doesn't recognize the words being prayed, the child can feel the love of its mother, and through her love, reach the Father. That means the attitude of your small baby holding your hands may communicate much more than words. Remember, your outward body reflects your inward spirit.

Lord, may my outward words communicate the
feelings and desires of my heart. And when
I can't put my desires into words, look
into my heart, and give me what I need.

8. *Don't teach them that God hears only because of posture.*

I've said that you can fold a young child's hands, kneel, bow your head, or even lift your head to look to Heaven when you pray. I also said you should have children close their eyes so they won't be distracted. These are only outward symbols that reflect an inner attitude toward God. However, make sure in your enthusiasm that you don't teach the wrong emphasis in prayer. While these "postures" are beneficial, children can wrongly put all their attention on the outer form and forget the inner meaning.

Prayer is relationship, so everything a child does in getting ready for prayer should point them to their inner relationship with God.

What else can your children do? They can get under the covers on a chilly evening and pray with a blanket pulled up around their neck. You can stand at the window and look to Heaven as the two of you pray. You can take a stroll outside to point out things in nature that you're thankful for—icicles, colored fall leaves, first flowers of spring, a squirrel, bird, or acorns. Challenge them, "How many things can we see that makes us thank God?"

You can sit on the porch or sun deck together. Sometimes you may pray with them sitting at the table before or after a meal.

9. *Teach your children to pray audibly.*

There were times in the Bible when God spoke *inwardly* to His people, giving them an inward impression of what He wanted them to do. But most of the time, God spoke in an audible voice to His people; that way, they could not mistake what God was saying. Isn't speaking out loud a good thing to teach your children? Shouldn't they be taught that God can't mistake what they are asking if they pray out loud?

It's very helpful for children to memorize Bible verses, then to quote them before their prayer, and use them in their prayer. Also, it's important for children to memorize prayers, and repeat them when praying. (See Chapter 11.) Just as two people speak audibly to communicate to one another, so teach your children to speak audibly to God, not so He will know what they want, but so you will know. Remind your children that sometimes a grunt or the nod of a head may get across the simplest of requests, but not much can be said beyond a grunt or nod.

Teach children to pray audibly for what they want, but also teach them they don't have to continually repeat the same thing over and over. Jesus taught, *"But when you pray do not use vain repetitions"* (Matt. 6:7). Your children may not understand "vain repetitions" so perhaps you can use the words of the New Living Translation, *"When you pray, don't babble on and on"* (Matt. 6:7 NLT). Remind children that they only have to ask one time for a chocolate chip cookie and you'll give it to them. In the same way, they only have to ask God one time, and He will hear and give them what they request.

> *Lord, You hear every muffled prayer when*
> *prayed from the heart, yet prayer is*
> *more effective when two agree in prayer.*

10. Teach them to pray so you can hear.

Sometimes children will bury their faces in a pillow or the covers and you don't hear or discern what they are saying. In one sense you don't need to hear and discern for their prayers to be effective, but on the other hand, Jesus taught that there is power when "two agree." *"Again I say to you that if two of you agree on earth concerning anything that they ask, it will be done for them by My Father in heaven"* (Matt. 18:19). You need to hear what your children pray to join in with their faith and fellowship with God.

Tell them, "If I can hear you, I can talk to God with you." Therefore, help them speak loudly enough, clearly enough, and distinctly enough. When you teach them to pray this way, you are also teaching them basic elements of communication that will help them in every area of life.

> *Lord, I love to pray both privately and with others.*
> *I learn much when I pray alone, and it's effective.*
> *I learn much when I pray with others, and it*
> *too is effective. I will spend my life doing both.*

11. Teach children to walk on both their right and left legs.

One leg is private prayers; your children must learn to pray by themselves. The other leg is praying publicly with others. Your children should learn to pray both with you audibly and pray privately. As we pray with another (whether a parent or someone else), we learn to pray better, and pray with faith, and pray sincerely—we learn much of what we need to know about prayer when we pray with others. As we pray privately, we grow in our intimate relationship with God.

Remember, as we walk forward, we walk right, left, right, left, right. To move forward spiritually, it's pray by yourself, pray with others, pray by yourself, pray with others.

Lord,
I will pray on both my right and left legs.

12. Teach them Christian music to create an atmosphere of prayer.

Just as churches may use an organ and/or piano to create a deep reverential spirit or a praise band to create a happy spirit, you too can use Christian music to prepare for prayer time. There are all types of music that your children may enjoy listening to on their iPod or CD players.

Good Christian music may point your children to the Bible, focus your children's attention on God, or in a general sense, prepare them for prayer. Use music to speak to your children, and through music motivate them to talk to God.

13. Teach the meaning behind memorized prayers.

It's all right to teach children how to memorize prayers (see Appendix A). But let them know when they pray something from memory, it's only a tool to help them remember. Prayer is not a formula, it's a relationship. Make sure they understand they're talking to God and telling God how they feel and telling God what they want. Prayer can be the genuine expression of a child-like love and faith in God. When you repeat a memorized prayer for your children and with your children, make sure you reflect the meaning of the words, showing them that prayer is relationship—not a formula.

Actual Prayers

Lord, remind me that the feelings of my heart come out
in words, and my love for You comes out in prayer.

14. Listen intently as your children pray.

If you want your children to pray later in life, make sure they pray when they are young. You should listen to them as they pray, as well as join them in their requests to God. Jesus tells us, *"if two of you shall agree as touching anything"* (Matt. 18:19 KJV). Usually we think of "two agreeing" as two adults. But what's wrong with believing it's you and your children agreeing together?

When your children are young, listen to them while they pray. Soon they will be older and praying, and praying for us more intelligently—even then we will be listening to them.

> *Lord, my children are so different. Help me*
> *to know each one intimately, to love each one*
> *completely, and teach them at their point of need.*

15. Let each child pray in his own unique way.

You already know by now that every child is a unique individual, different from all the other children in your family, or your extended family. As a result, he or she will naturally express their prayers different from other members in the family. So you have a great challenge to help each child pray in his or her point of need and interest. The most important part is that they connect to God in conversation.

Remember, your efforts to educate your children will need to be tailored to their different types of motivation. The same with prayer; you should ask God in your private prayers to help you see the difference in your children, learn how to motivate them differently, and learn how to help them pray according to their own differences.

Here's a tip. Try to identify each child with a person in the Bible. Remember, people in the Bible were very different. Notice that David the shepherd was also a musician; Solomon liked to study animals and nature; Dorcas liked to sew; Cain liked to grow vegetables (just because he sinned does not violate his attitude toward agriculture); and his brother Abel liked to raise animals. Haven't you known the child who loves pets more than another child who loves science and experimentation, and another who loves to tinker with electronic things? You should attempt to connect with your children according to their needs, and point their hearts to God in prayer.

16. Say "talking to God" as often as you can rather than the word "prayer."

There's nothing wrong with using the word *prayer*, but there were many other synonyms in the Bible for prayer—asking, praising, magnifying, worshiping, begging, and making known. But *talking to God* is a picture that children understand. When they talk to God it puts them in a personal relationship with God.

Lord, forgive me when I make prayers hard
and cumbersome. May I always talk to
You simply from the sincerity of my heart.

17. Make it easy to talk to God.

When your children begin to pray, don't try to force big words on them. When they are young they will not understand all the biblical words associated with prayer. Make prayer as easy as possible, so that there's no barrier between them and God.

If you use big words when you talk to God in their presence, they begin to think that their prayers aren't worthy or as important. Whatever you do, don't tell your children with your body

136

language, facial expression, or correction, that you disapprove of the language they use in prayers.

*Lord, teach me the simplicity of prayer and
teach me to use simple words when I talk to You.*

18. Don't pray using King James English.

"Oh, Thou almighty God, we come into Thy hallowed presence." While King James English was correct for its day, using this type of language today may have some unwanted results. First, you may turn children off to prayer because they don't recognize or use that language. Second, they may pray hypercritically using the King James English. Third, you teach a false concept of prayer language for them today, and you take away the intimate relationship with God that they can have.

Instead of lofty prose, have them pray, "Lord, I scraped my knee," or "Forgive me for making my sister mad," or "Help me write my report."

*Lord, help me see "ruts" in my life before I begin
to help my children with ruts in their lives.*

19. When your children fall into a "prayer rut," help them climb out.

What is a *prayer rut?* A prayer rut is when a child prays the same thing every night. A prayer rut could be, "Now I lay me down to sleep, I pray the Lord my soul to keep, if I should die…" Get them out of the rut by helping them recognize what they are praying in each of those requests. Sometimes you have to ask them to explain the words they use, or ask them for another word that means the same thing. Get them to pray in their own words.

Also, when your children get into the rut of "bless momma... bless father...bless sister...bless grandpa...," have them stop and pray a specific request for each one for whom they prayed. Or think together about a special praise for each one for whom they prayed, or thank God for doing something in their lives.

20. *Don't let their prayers be one-sided.*

By one-sided we mean don't let them just ask God to "bless" people every night. Teach your children to ask for things for them, to praise God for His work in their lives, to use those people, or to worship God for His greatness and goodness to them.

Anyone may become one-sided in their prayers from time to time. Children will do that because it's only natural. So begin by example, if you find yourself in a one-sided prayer, point out to the child what you've been doing, and tell them you're going to broaden your prayer. This is a way of teaching them to follow your example. At certain times you may want to spend time thanking God for His answers, and other times you may want to praise God for what He has done in their lives.

21. *Teach them to dedicate their whole body to God.*

Some nights, tell your children that tonight they are going to have a dedication service. They may not understand the word *dedication* depending on their ages, but tell them they're going to give every part of themselves to God. Lead the children to give God their feet, hands, eyes, mouths, ears, and finally their hearts.

Lord, I will start now to pray with my children
and I will keep it up. Help me make up for lost
time and use my available time left with them.

22. Early in their lives, teach your children how to pray, and keep it up.

If you pray with your children only once or twice a week, that's better than not praying at all. If you waited to start praying with them until they were in the fourth or sixth grade, that's better than not having done it at all.

But if possible, begin praying with your children before they can talk. Then as they eat, help them say a simple prayer such as, "Thank You for food." Then when they get older you can teach them, "God is great, God is good, let us thank Him for our food. By His hands we all are fed, let us thank Him for our daily bread."

Our strategy is to start early, and as they grow in language ability, so will they grow to express their prayers in a broader context and more specific requests.

We should look for growth in the prayers of our children as they go through elementary school, middle school, and into high school.

Lord, forgive me when I make prayer a
"habit." May I always come to You
because of my need of Your greatness.

23. Teach life habits.

A child asks, "Will I have to say my prayers for the rest of my life?" Interesting question. It might come from a child who is bored or his prayers are not meaningful. Then answer like this: "You'll have to brush your teeth and take a bath, and eat three meals the rest of your life. You will want to pray every day not because you have to, but because you will want to—because it's enjoyable. Don't you look forward to eating a delicious meal each evening?"

"Yes!"

"Prayer is something that you'll also enjoy nightly."

Parents often talk about the younger generation as if they didn't have anything to do with it.

—Haim Ginott

(http://www.quotegarden.com/parents.html)

These are the commands, decrees, and regulations
that the Lord your God commanded me to teach
you. You must obey them in the land you are about
to enter and occupy, and you and your children and grandchil-
dren must fear the Lord your God as
long as you live. If you obey all his decrees and
commands, you will enjoy a long life. Listen
closely, Israel, and be careful to obey. Then all will
go well with you, and you will have many children
in the land flowing with milk and honey, just as
the Lord, the God of your ancestors, promised you.

Listen, O Israel! The Lord is our God, the Lord
alone. And you must love the Lord your God with
all your heart, all your soul, and all your strength.
And you must commit yourselves wholeheartedly
to these commands that I am giving you today"
(Deuteronomy 6:1-6 NLT).

CHAPTER 10

How to Bless Children

Lord, I want my children, and my children's
children to have Your full blessing in their
lives. Teach me how to better bless them.

In the fall of 1994, I (Elmer) spoke to a minister's convention
in West Virginia. The chairman of the State Board of Christian
Education, Reverend Vondie Cook II, was not able to meet me on
Friday night for dinner, his wife was in the labor delivery room;
she had just given birth to their son, Chance. I understood and
had dinner alone. As I blessed the food before eating, I prayed
God's blessing on his wife and the child.

The next morning Vondie Cook met me early at the convention center in Beckley, West Virginia, and got the meeting started, but explained that he would leave during the morning to pick up his wife and new son. She was leaving the hospital less than 24 hours after their son was born. We had a wonderful morning convention.

After lunch, I had just started my presentation, when looking down the aisle into the foyer I saw Vondie and a woman I assumed to be his wife. He was "proud as a peacock," holding a bundle that I knew was his newborn baby. I yelled, "Come on in, let's have a look at that baby." As Pastor Cook walked to the front, the audience broke into applause, and then I announced, "We're going to dedicate this baby to God." I invited the grandmother and grandfather (he is also a minister) to also come forward for the dedication. Then taking the baby with two hands, I held the child high to God and prayed,

> God, our Lord, we offer Chance to You and dedicate him to be Your servant. He has a wonderful father and grandfather who have served You in ministry. Lord, we pray that Chance would serve You with the same amount of dedication, whether in fulltime ministry or wherever You call him. I dedicate Chance to You that he would come to trust in You early and understand his salvation and walk in the fullness of Jesus Christ. I dedicate Chance to a life of holiness and service.
>
> Lord, I pray that You would keep Chance from the evil one who would destroy his life. Help him to grow, to learn many lessons, fill him with wisdom and knowledge. Help him to understand the spiritual world, and live in the heavenlies. May Chance grow up in the church and

144

grow up to attend church and may he love the preaching of Your Word in the local church.

Bless Pastor Vondie, his father, that he would raise his son in Your nurture and admonition. Make him a good father. We dedicate Vondie and Teresa to you today for this great task to raise this new baby for Your glory.

We dedicate Reverend and Mrs. Cook to You as grand-parents. May they be great examples, wise in counsel, and may they be used in the life of Chance to accomplish Your purpose.

What You Need to Know

1. **God wants to bless children.**

2. **God can use you to bless them.**

3. **You must be blessed before you can bless them.**

4. **God has a formula for you to follow to bless them.**

5. **A child has added value when blessed.**

Blessing Children

Not everyone who tells a child, "God bless you" or who bless-es a child adds value to the little one. God has a formula for you to follow when blessing a child. You should follow that formula to get the best results.

Lord,
I want to find that formula
and use it to bless my children.

145

Don't be disturbed that God has a formula that you must follow to bless children. There are a lot of things in life that demand a formula. Take my laptop computer for example. I must use the correct password to get access to the files on it and to the Internet. Only my administrative assistant and I know that phrase; when we follow the right formula, the world of the Internet opens up to us. So if you've tried to bless a child, and nothing happens—you think—look at God's formula. Follow it!

You must have the right key to get the door to open, the right number to reach someone on your cell phone, the right code to reach your voice mail, the right remote control signal to open your garage door, and the right address to get a letter delivered. So why should we be amazed to find out that God has the right formula for us to follow when we bless another?

Perhaps the best is a five-step formula found in the book, *The Gift of Blessing* by Gary Smalley and John Trent.[1]

The blessing includes:

1. **A meaningful touch.**

2. **A spoken word.**

3. **Attaching "high value" to the one being blessed.**

4. **Picturing a special future for the one being blessed.**

5. **An active commitment to fulfill the blessing.**

> *Lord, thank You for this formula. As I read more about it, help me to understand and apply it to my family.*

When you follow these five steps, you may have more success in blessing others. Why? Because God wants to bless people, and He wants to use His children to bless others, but we must follow a biblical suggestion to bless others. When you follow the formula, you can add value to other lives as you bless them.

Lord, open my eyes as I read and show me
how to bless children. Give me a passion to
bless children and teach me how to do it.

A meaningful touch suggests that you touch the person you're blessing, which may be a catch-22. Why? Because if you touch a member of the opposite sex, that person may misunderstand, or an observer may think you are taking a sexual liberty. Also, in this day of liberal litigation, people may think that touching a child involves child abuse, or taking advantage of a child. So if you hold a child or place your hand heavily on the head of a child when blessing him or her, your actions may be misunderstood.

During baby dedication at my church for Bradford Elmer Towns, my grandson/namesake, I (Elmer) placed my hand on his head as the pastor prayed. My grandson would have none of that, constantly trying to push my hand away or wriggling his head from out underneath my hand. He was much too young to understand the intent of a blessing. Others around me understood what was happening, even though they chuckled because they thought he was cute.

- *An embrace.* Biblical counselors have given several illustrations of young people who were emotionally stunted because they grew up without the loving embrace of either parents, or one parent. Some have emotional difficulty simply because they did not experience the acceptance of their parents through a loving embrace. That's because the embrace signifies belongingness, value, and "you're special." Every child growing up needs to feel special in the eyes of his or her parents. Remember the time you fell down and ran to your mother for an embrace? Suddenly, your world felt better. An embrace adds value to their life, which is another description for blessing.

Lord, help me embrace my children
spiritually, as I embrace them physically.

Sometimes an embrace is a *natural blessing*. Your daughter completes her piano recital and as she skips up to you afterward, you give her a hug. It makes no difference if she did well or not. You embrace her because she's yours and she needs affirmation. On other occasion, an embrace conveys a *spiritual blessing*. Perhaps you've just prayed with a child, then you gave him or her a big hug. Perhaps a child has made a decision for God, or has correctly repeated a verse. Your big hug is a spiritual affirmation. You've told the child that you accept him or her as he or she seeks to serve the Lord.

Lord, as I embrace Your love, I will
embrace my children so they feel Your love.

- *Convey the blessing with a kiss.* When Isaac wanted to bless his son, he said, *"Come near now and kiss me, my son"* (Gen. 27:26). A father conveys love upon his son with kiss. There is perhaps no greater emotional expression to your children than the kiss.

- *Convey the blessing by holding.* It's a special time when a grandfather picks up his grandchild and places him on his knee. The grandfather blesses his child by telling him all the great things that they will do on this earth or do for God. Sitting on a lap, the child will receive a deeper message than if the child only hears it with his or her ears. To be held on Grandpa's lap identifies the child with the past ages, because the child has reached beyond his or her own natural father. I remember my grandpa Robert Eli McFadden Jr., hoisting me up onto his red mule, and we galloped across a plowed field, racing the mail delivery man to the rural mailbox. We laughed all the way, what a great experience for a grandson and grandfather. I think I must have been three or four years old. Later that night he hoisted me onto his knee in front of a roaring open fire in his bedroom and sang, "De Camptown ladies sing dis song—Doo-dah! doo-dah!..." I don't know if this was his favorite song, but it's the only one I ever remember my grandfather singing to me. So what do I remember about my grandfather? That I liked him and he liked me. I remember feeling special.

Even Jesus held the children as He blessed them, *"And He [Jesus] took them up in His arms, laid His hands on them, and blessed them"* (Mark 10:16). What better example to convey blessing upon children than to do it as Jesus did.

Lord, I want to embrace and bless my children, just as You did when You were on earth.

149

- *Touching the head to bless.* I (Elmer) do this quite often when I bless a baby. I place my hand on the child's head and pray God's blessing upon the child. Yesterday (as I write this chapter), Connie Nylander, a former secretary in the Religion department at Liberty University, brought her infant daughter McKenna Grace to the office. She reminded me that I had blessed McKenna when she was only a few days old. I blessed little McKenna Grace when she was first born, and then again when she was 10 months old. I picked her up, and placing my hand on her head, blessed her again. Why did I do that? Because I believe God answers prayer, and will bless with added value little McKenna simply because I prayed blessings upon her. But I also prayed that God would keep her from the evil one. Protection is an essential part of the blessing. Then I prayed that McKenna would accept Christ when she came of age. One of the reasons I know God will bless this child in answer to prayer, is because her mother Connie is a godly young woman who prays for McKenna. Then again, I know God will bless McKenna because the Lord promised, *"That if two of you shall agree on earth as touching any thing that they shall ask, it shall be done for them of my Father which is in heaven"* (Matt. 18:19 KJV). Connie and I joined together to "ask" God's blessing on McKenna.

In Scriptures we have the illustration of Jacob placing his hands on the heads of his two grandsons as he blessed them. *"Then Israel [Jacob] stretched out his right hand and laid it on Ephraim's head...and his left hand on Manasseh's head"* (Gen. 48:14). Blessing with a touch was an act of faith, because the writer of Hebrews indicated, *"It was by faith that Jacob, when he was old and dying, blessed each of Joseph's sons"* (Heb. 11:21 LB).

> *Lord, use me to bless children as I lay*
> *my hands on their heads and bless them.*

- *Other ways to a meaningful touch in blessing.* You also tell a person that they are valuable with a hand-shake or when you reach out to hold hands as you pray-bless them. Holding hands may be a way to add value to their life. You're telling them they are "special" just by touching them.

In Bible times, people seem to be more emotional than we are today. They hugged, kissed, embraced, and held one another. In a day when it's politically incorrect to touch a child, your actions and desires must be above suspicion. When you do it, make sure you have the approval of parents or other supervising adults. There are Bible illustrations of meaningfully touching a child in love and acceptance, to build up the child's ego and self-perception.

> *Lord, I will bless my children from my*
> *heart so they feel my love for them.*

Blessing With a Spoken Word

God has chosen to use the "spoken word" to bless a person. The person who hears you bless them receives *added* value—natural blessing because they know you affirm them, and spiritual blessing because you pray for them. Also, the spoken word adds

151

the power of faith when you speak (see Mark 11:23). Some might suggest you don't need to "speak" a blessing, that you can privately pray or bless a person and God will respond by *adding* value to their life. Certainly your private intercession will touch the life of the person you blessed; however, emphasis is made in the Bible on "speaking the blessing." God instructed the priests how to bless Israel, *"...saying unto them, 'The Lord bless thee...'"* (Num. 6:23-24 KJV). Notice what God said the blessing included, *"They [the priests] shall put my name upon the children of Israel; and I will bless them'"* (Num. 6:27 KJV). The priests must speak the blessing they want on the people and verbally say the name of the Lord upon the people.

> *Lord, I will speak Your Word over my children*
> *so they remember what You've said to them.*

Why is speaking the blessing important? First, because what's in a person's heart comes out of the mouth (see Matt. 15:18) or as the old farmer said, "What's in the well, comes up in the bucket." Even God wanted a convert to say with his mouth, *"That Jesus is the Lord"* (1 Cor. 12:3 KJV). So when you speak a blessing, what you really want God to do, must come out of the depth of your heart in your speech.

Second, when you say a blessing over a person, they hear what you have said. You put your faith on the spot, as well as putting God on the spot. A spoken blessing is an active expression of faith. Jesus told His disciples to speak what they want, *"...whosoever shall say unto this mountain, be thou removed...shall have whatsoever he saith"* (Mark 11:23 KJV). In this example, Jesus connects your spoken word to divine accomplishment. Therefore, you must not just think a blessing silently, nor pray a blessing inwardly, you must speak audible the blessing because your words activate your faith, and belief delivers what you speak.

But a third thing happens when you speak and they hear the blessing—the two of you have "agreed together." God uses agreement because it is outward, expectant, and honoring to God, *"Again I say unto you, That if two of you shall agree on earth as touching any thing that they shall ask, it shall be done for them of my Father which is in heaven"* (Matt. 18:19 KJV). When you pray a blessing—in agreement—you receive the blessing you pray.

Notice how faith was tied to Isaac's blessing to his son. *"By faith, Isaac blessed Jacob"* (Heb. 11:20 KJV). Remember, Isaac was living in tents in the desert. He had no land inheritance to give his son and only meager resources for an inheritance. But, Isaac had faith that God would keep His promise made to him and to Abraham by multiplying Jacob's seed physically and spiritually. So in the blessing Isaac said to Jacob, *"...Thou shalt not take a wife of the daughters of Canaan"* (Gen. 28:1 KJV), the blessing involved a condition that Isaac was to be separated from sin, the sinful tribes surrounding them. Second, Isaac was told, *"...take thee a wife from thence of the daughters of Laban thy mother's brother"* (Gen. 28:2 KJV). This condition to receive the blessing of God related to whom he must marry. The blessing on Jacob was reflected in holiness, he had to be separated unto God.

*Lord, I will let my children know what
I want them to do when I bless them.*

But there is another aspect of Isaac's blessing to Jacob. *"God Almighty bless thee, and make thee fruitful, and multiply thee, that thou mayest be a multitude of people"* (Gen. 28:3 KJV). Here Isaac is predicting a blessing that his son would be a mighty nation. When

Isaac spoke this blessing, there were probably only two or three dozen people in Isaac's camp. The father's blessing of prosperity upon his son involved outward faith, not just faith secreted in his heart; but faith spoken so that all could hear—that Jacob would become a mighty nation.

So when you bless, speak outwardly for both you and the recipient to hear. And when you bless children, not only should they hear what you say, make sure that the parents, grandparents, and those who influence the children also hear what you predict-bless.

Lord, I will speak Your words over
my children when I bless them.

- *The influence of the tongue in blessing.* God continually reminds us that our tongue controls our life. The Bible describes the tongue like a bridle in a horse's mouth that guides a powerful horse where it shall go, and like a small rudder on a mighty ship, it turns it about. So our tongue directs our life. Notice what James said, *"But the tongue can no man tame; it is an unruly evil, full of deadly poison. Therewith bless we God, even the Father; and therewith curse we men..."* (James 3:8-9 KJV). You can bless children with your tongue, or hurt them.

Why your blessings may not work:

1. You haven't been blessed.

2. You don't bless in faith.

3. You don't follow God's formula.

154

4.   You bless the wrong way.

5.   You bless the wrong person.

Because our words are our life. When we bless with our mouth, we pledge our life to the one we bless. When a baby is brought before a church in dedication, the parents pledge to raise that baby in the "nurture and admonition of the Lord." The pastor pledges the church's support to raise that child and all "agree together," asking God to bless the child. But they go further, each pledge with all their power might bring about God's blessing upon the child.

Counselors Smalley and Trent give several illustrations of how our words influence our children. By constant criticism we tear down their self-esteem and make children feel insignificant or of little value. But when we praise our children, we add value to their lives. When you pray for children, you raise their level of expectation and you add your expectation that you think they can do it.

As a small boy, my mother took me (Elmer) to her family graveyard near Sardinia, South Carolina, where stood a large 10-foot granite stone that lists the original members of her McFadden family that settled the area in 1732. The stone listed each generation from John McFadden to the present. The McFadden Stone was a symbol of family pride, stability, and a challenge to do what they did. My mother said to me, "Remember who you are; make me proud of you." As I stood before that massive stone, I felt the heavy obligation of my forefathers upon my young shoulders. My mother would say, "Remember who you are; you can do anything you put your mind to doing." She was setting the bar of expectations high. Now I've not been able to do all I want to do, but that doesn't mean I didn't try. My mother did not call what she did to me "the blessing," but she passed on to me family expectations. It had the same impact of a blessing.

Lord,
I will bless my children with the
expectations I have for them. Then, I
will pray that they accomplish what I bless.

Your words can tear down your children's self-esteem and handcuff them in their future. When you tell a child, "Your room is always dirty," you make them seem less valued in your eyes and theirs. When you tell a child, "You're not as smart as your sister," or "You're so clumsy," what have you said to the child? You've told that child, "You're a loser."

My friend John Maxwell says that we put symbolic numbers on their forehead. When you tear down a child by saying, "You're always dirty," you put a number "one" or a "two" upon their forehead. When you praise a child for an outstanding term paper or when their team wins a Little League game, you're putting a "nine" or a "ten" upon their forehead.

Now while I don't like the illustration of playing poker, life is sometimes like a card game. Every time you tell a child he is dirty, dumb, a failure, you're like a dealer of cards, dealing that child a "loser card." And when children spend their lives gathering "loser cards," what happens when they get ready to get into life's games? If all the children are holding are "loser cards," usually they fold. To be a winner in poker, you've got to have "winner cards." And what are "winner cards?" When you say to a child, "That's wonderful...you're great...that looks cute on you...congratulations...those are "winner cards."

Why we don't praise:

1. We feel it will take away their motivation.

2. We feel it inflates their ego.

3. We feel uncomfortable doing it.

4. We don't mean it.

5. We think they know it without our saying it.

6. Our parents didn't praise us.

7. We think they will take advantage of us.

There are many excuses you can give for not using praise-words with the young. For whatever reason you can think of, it doesn't have any weight compared to the opposite of what you've accomplished. When you use words of praise or blessing, you build them up, you prepare them for the future, and you make them solid believers.

Lord, I will bless my children with praise
and commendation. Use my words
to build in them a strong urge to serve You.

Attach High Value to the One Blessed

When you bless someone, you are giving that person high importance in your sight. Also, when you speak God's name over a person, you're giving him or her importance in God's sight. If you love your children, they will know it. When you bless them with words, they'll feel it.

The word bless in Hebrew means "to bow the knee." So when you bow to a king, you are indicating that his importance has become important to you. So when you bless people, you are saying that they are now important to you. What do you do by putting a "10" on people's foreheads? You are making them important to you, and you create a *special relationship* between them and God.

> *Lord,*
> *I will make my children feel important.*

After a terrible disaster, a father ran through cut glass and twisted corrugated roofing, looking for his son. Afterward as his feet were being bandaged, the father was asked, "Didn't you feel the lacerations on your feet?" He answered, "No, I was holding my boy." How precious are your children to you?

Jacob blessed his son Judah saying that Judah was a young lion (see Gen. 49:9). What did he mean when he called Judah a young lion? It's the same thing today when a hard-driving young businessman is called a "young lion." The same thing when a new, extremely aggressive football player has a will to win. When you call someone a *young lion*, you are predicting a certain way to succeed in life. A young lion will achieve by strength, aggression, and ability.

When Jacob blessed another son, "Issachar is a strong donkey" (Gen. 49:14), what was he saying about this son? Since a donkey is the burden-bearer, the worker, the one that can be counted on, Jacob is saying that Issachar as a faithful son would carry his burdens of responsibility. Others could count on Issachar, and even Issachar himself would bear the burdens of others. We like to have people like Issachar around because they solve our problems, they make life easier for us, they are a blessing to all. Some may blush at calling a son a donkey. But if you examine this carefully, calling Issachar a donkey was a blessing that predicted his future. As Issachar grew older, he tried to live up to his father's expectations by being faithful, helping others, and adding value to everyone around him.

When Jacob blessed, "Napthali, he is a young deer," what was he saying about the future of this son? Jacob was saying that "Napthali was beautiful, because everyone appreciates the grace and form of a young deer, whether running through the field or drinking silently at a stream." Jacob was saying to his son, "You will do things right, other people will admire you; you are artistic, appropriate, and picturesque." When Jacob pointed out this potential in his son, obviously Napthali tried to fulfill that prediction. Hence, the blessing given by his father became a reality in life.

Shortly after his baptism, Jesus was introduced to Simon Peter. When Jesus first met the husky fisherman, He said, *"You are Simon the son of Jonah"* (John 1:42). The Greek word *Simon* comes from the Hebrew word *Simeon* which means "listener." Peter's parents named him Simeon when he was born. But if anything, Peter never listened to anyone. Peter was blunt, strong, and self-reliant. A listener...no!

So when Jesus met Simeon He said, "You shall be called Cephas (which is translated A Stone)" (John 1:42). Jesus gave him a new name—*rock*. And when you think of a rock, what comes to mind—dependable, solid, firm? While giving him a new name was not a technical blessing, it was a prediction of what he was to become. On several occasions Peter was flexible and weak. The Master had to rebuke Peter for telling Him not to go to Jerusalem and again Jesus rebuked him because of his braggadocios attitude, claiming he would never deny the Lord. Peter failed, he was no rock on that occasion. But when the Lord needed a solid man to introduce the Church on the Day of Pentecost before a large hostile crowd of bigoted Jews, Jesus chose Peter to be the spokesman. Why? Because Peter was a rock. He had become the name Jesus gave him.

Lord, I will bless my children with good
expectations, then I will pray for
my blessings to come true in their lives.

Picturing a Special Future for the One Blessed

When you bless someone, you are not dealing with the past, and probably not the present. You are pointing them toward the future. When Isaac blessed Jacob, he pointed out how God would use him in the future. Isaac blessed him (Jacob)… *"Let people serve thee, and nations bow down to thee: be lord over thy brethren, and let thy mother's sons bow down to thee…"* (Gen. 27:29 KJV). God had chosen Jacob to be the father of the 12 tribes of Israel. So when Isaac blessed Jacob, he was predicting that he would be a leader over his brothers and the family would bow to him. What a special future!

When John Maxwell became a grandfather, he gave his granddaughter a special name, *Sunshine.* He was telling everyone his granddaughter brought special joy to his life. Don't you think the granddaughter would always try to bring joy to the life of her grandfather?

160

How to Bless Children

Lord, May we all bless the children
who bring joy to our lives.

When you bless a child, try to make it open-ended. Just as water cannot rise above its source, so children usually do not rise above the expectations we put upon them. When you say to a child, "You'll never be much of a ball player," you may be limiting that child's future. While some use negative motivation to try to bring about the best in a child, be careful that you don't put so much baggage on the child that you kill the child's initiative. It is possible to allow too much sun that you burn up a flower, or that you put too much water on the flower, so that you drown it. In the same way, it is possible to give too many compliments to your child, or to be too critical. Isn't balance the key to life?

Your expectations when blessing should be consistent with both your past actions and theirs. When a young boy shows promise in sports, praise that boy by reminding him of all the things he does well. When a young girl shows excellence in caring for others, point out her mercy, challenging her to be a doctor or nurse.

Don't be so foolish as to bless a child toward a goal that is unreachable or unmanageable. For the young man in braces with polio, don't challenge him to the area of running. And for the young child who has little ability in science or schoolwork, don't challenge him to be a medical doctor or a Ph.D. Be realistic! Since blessing is adding value to a life, challenge them to the next goal in life that is attainable.

Lord, give me wisdom to challenge
my children to obtainable goals.

161

An Active Commitment to Fulfill the Blessing

When you bless someone, you are making a commitment to that person. This means you shouldn't walk through the mall trying to lay your hand in blessing on every person you see—you can't help carry out the blessing you give. When you bless a person, it should be because you have a relationship with that person. Through that relationship, you will help them reach the blessing you speak.

When I walk through my Sunday school class before it begins, I say to many people, "God bless you." Is that an empty formula? I hope not, for I have committed myself to help by teaching them the Word of God. I have committed my teaching to help them live by biblical principles. So when I say, "God bless you," I know I've made a commitment to help them receive the blessing that I speak.

- *You do something involved with the blessing.* When you bless someone, you have an obligation to help accomplish what you have spoken. When a grandfather blesses his grandchildren to receive education, or to "be the best you can be," what should a grandfather do? He should take time to teach his grandchildren, or pass values onto them, or put money into an account to help them go to college.

Just to walk by someone and say, "God bless you," without following up with your good works, does not fit God's formula. *"If a brother or sister be naked, or destitute…and you say unto them, 'God bless you,' but do not give them anything, what good is that?"* (James 2:15-16, author's translation). Your blessing is empty when you pray God's blessing on a person but do nothing to fulfill your prayer.

Lord, keep me from hypocritical blessings
when I don't do anything to help the one I blessed.

- *A blessing is sharing what God has given you.* Jacob had been blessed of God. His father Isaac said to him, *"May God give you of the dew of heaven"* (Gen. 27:28). This was symbolic of prosperity God would put upon the things Jacob's hand would touch. Many years later when Jacob came to blessing his grandsons he said, *"The God who has been my shepherd...bless you"* (see Gen. 48:15-16). Just as a shepherd lives outdoors with his sheep experiencing the dew of Heaven, now Jacob was blessing his grandchildren with the same blessing.

- *A blessing involves their best interest.* When you are blessing someone, it is not for your own good; but rather you are *adding value* to their life. Sometimes in ministry, it could be deceptive to bless the people to whom you minister because you want to bless them just to make you more successful. Will God honor that motive? Probably not! You bless people for *their* best interest, what will prosper them.

As Jacob was blessing his grandchildren, notice how the blessing was described. *"He [Jacob] blessed them, each one with the blessing appropriate to him"* (Gen. 49:28 NASB). This means that when Jacob blessed his 12 sons, each one got a different blessing that was appropriate for his strength, his passion, or his future. So what does that mean? It means you must be wise, knowing the person that you are blessing.

Second, you must be insightful, understanding what people desire for the future, and how they plan to live for God.

And third, you must have deep faith that God can give the blessing for which you pray. Since everyone has an "appropriate blessing," learn what is appropriate for each person before you attempt to bless him or her.

Lord, teach me what I should know
when blessing my children.

- *Become a student of those you intend to bless.* Before you bless a person, you must know something about them. Otherwise, how can you make the blessing appropriate to them? Your blessing might be empty words. Have we not heard someone pray, "Lord, bless him..." What we didn't hear was what the blessing should accomplish in the child's life, or how the blessing was going to be accomplished. To speak a specific blessing, you must know the person, which means you must become a student of those you intend to bless.

What must you know? You must know a little bit about their nature and how they solve their problems. You must understand their dreams, the things they want to do in life. What about their potential? What are they good at? And where is their passion? Also, don't forget their spiritual gifts. Where has God given them ability to serve Him? All of these become a mix that determines what they want to do in life. Then when you know that, your blessing can give direction and meaning.

Lord, give me insight into my children
so I know what to bless in their lives.

- *Become a teacher to those you intend to bless.* You want to bless someone by pouring your life into him or her. Therefore, you must become a teacher to those you bless. *"Train up a child in the way he should go, and when he is old, he will not depart from it"* (Prov. 22:6). When the father speaks a blessing upon his son, commending him for his good play in Little League baseball, what else must the father do? Obviously, if he wants his son to be a winning sportsman, the father must take him to games, practice with him, build him up after defeats, and praise him after victories. If you want your son to be a winner, you must pour a winning attitude into him. Socrates said, "We give so little attention to training those, into whose hands we must ultimately commit all."

Lord, help me learn the following
ways to bless my children.

Suggestions for Learning How to Bless

The following questions give you a foundation on which to build blessings for your children.

1. How will you bless your children? Write what you will say and do. Will you place your hands on their heads, their shoulders, or will you hold them?

2. Why are your children valuable to you? Write your thoughts.

3. What things can you do today to "add value" to their lives? Make a list.

4. How do you feel about the formula for blessing your children? What aspects of the formula will you use?

Endnote

1. Gary Smalley and John Trent, *The Gift of Blessing* (Nashville: Thomas Nelson, 1993), 19.

There are two lasting bequests we can give our children. One is roots. The other is wings.

—Hodding Carter Jr.

(http://www.quotegarden.com/parents.html)

Susannah Wesley's 16 Rules

1. *Eating between meals not allowed.*

2. *As children they are to be in bed by 8 P.M.*

3. *They are required to take medicine without complaining.*

4. *Subdue self-will in a child, and those working together with God to save the child's soul.*

5. *To teach a child to pray as soon as he can speak.*

6. *Require all to be still during Family Worship.*

7. *Give them nothing that they cry for, and only that when asked for politely.*

8. *To prevent lying, punish no fault which is first confessed and repented of.*

9. *Never allow a sinful act to go unpunished.*

10. *Never punish a child twice for a single offense.*

11. *Comment and reward good behavior.*

12. *Any attempt to please, even if poorly performed, should be commended.*

13. Preserve property rights, even in smallest matters.

14. Strictly observe all promises.

15. Require no daughter to work before she can read well.

16. Teach children to fear the rod.

—Susannah Wesley

(http://www.familyofdestiny.com/article_16rules.htm)

CHAPTER 11

Practical Ideas and Prayers for Praying With Children

There are many "helps" that will assist you in praying to God for spiritual breakthrough for children. Some of the following are suggestions, others are memorized prayers. Try any of these or all of these.

Five-Finger Prayer

The five-finger prayer is a technique taught me by my son, Dr. Sam Towns, Associate Professor at Liberty University, who went to be home with the Lord in January 2002. On several occasions when he was "called" to give a devotion or impromptu talk, he would always hold up five fingers and talk about the five-finger prayer. Use this with your children.

1. *Your thumb is nearest you*, so begin by praying for those who are closest to you. These are the easiest to remember—mother, father, brother, sister, grandparents, aunts and uncles, cousins, and other relatives. Other people who are close to you are your close friends. To pray for our loved ones is, as C.S. Lewis once said, a "sweet duty."

2. *The next finger is the pointer.* Pray for those who teach, instruct, and heal. This includes teachers, doctors, ministers, etc. They need support and wisdom in pointing others in the right direction toward their heavenly Father.

3. *The third finger is tall man.* This reminds us of our leaders. We are to pray for our president, state, and local officials. Then pray for leaders in business and administrators. These are the people who shape our nation and guide public opinion. They need God's guidance.

4. *The fourth finger is ring finger.* Many people say that the ring finger is in fact the weakest of all our fingers, so pray for those who are weak, in trouble or pain. These involve sick relatives, and those who have been in accidents.

5. *The last finger is the small finger,* our pinky. It's the smallest place of all, and that's where we are. We should be small in the sight of God. So when we come to the last thing, we pray for ourselves. And when you think of the smallest finger, remember

what Jesus said, "He who is least shall be the greatest among you." The pinky should remind you to pray for yourself.

Be Near Me, Lord Jesus

Be near me, Lord Jesus! I ask Thee to stay close by me forever and love me, I pray. Bless all the dear children in Thy tender care and take us to Heaven to live with Thee there. Amen.[1]

Mom and Dad's Blessing for a New Child

Thank you, Lord, for the precious gift of this child. Because Your Word says that every good gift comes from You, I know that You have given him (her) to me to care for and raise. Help me to do that. Show me places where I continue to hang on to him (her) and enable me to release him (her) to Your protection, guidance, and counsel. Help me not to live in fear of possible dangers, but in the joy and peace of knowing that You are in control.

*I'm grateful that I don't have to rely on the world's unreliable and ever-changing methods for child rearing, but that I can have clear directions from Your word and wisdom as I pray to You for answers. I rely on You for everything, and this day I trust my child to You and release him (her) into Your hands.
Amen.*

—Stormie Omartian, *The Power of a Praying Parent*[2]

*We receive this child from You Lord, knowing You
have formed its body, personality, and inner spirit.
We bless this gift of life with our love and gratitude.*

*We acknowledge Your sovereignty over this
child and our family, knowing You placed this
child here to teach us as we in turn teach
him/her how to live together in love.
We bless this child with the gift of family.*

*We accept our duty to teach this child about
You, how to live for You, and how to live
and make a living in this world.
We bless this child with our example and instruction.*

*We promise to protect this child from spiritual danger,
as well as from physical threats and wants.
We bless this child with a protective hedge of prayer
and the provision of physical necessities.*

*We commit ourselves to be godly examples as parents,
and devoted followers of Jesus Christ.
We bless this child with our faith and guidance.*

*Lord, help us to bless this child by fulfilling
the promises we make today.
Amen![3]*

The Ultimate Blessing of Children

Of all the blessings I can give you,
May you know Christ and have eternal life.

Of all the blessings that will guide your life,
May you be blameless in character and live for Christ.

Of all the wealth I can bless you with,
May you have a spirit to work hard, a
spirit of excellence in work, and a spirit of
happiness in each job well done.

Of all the protection I can bless upon you,
May you receive God's will and live
under the protection He gives.

Of all the marriage blessings I can give,
May you marry well, may you fulfill your life in your
family and may God's love be reflected on
your love for your mate.
Amen.[4]

Children's Morning Prayer

Lord, in the morning I start each day,
By taking a moment to bow and pray.
I start with thanks, and then give praise
For all your kind and loving ways.

Today if sunshine turns to rain,
If a dark cloud brings some pain,

175

I won't doubt or hide in fear
For you, my God, are always near.

I will travel where you lead;
I will help my friends in need.
Where you send me I will go;
With your help I'll learn and grow.

Hold my family in your hands,
As we follow your commands.
And I will keep you close in sight
Until I crawl in bed tonight.
Amen.

—Mary Fairchild[5]

O Lord, my God, to Thee I pray
While from my bed I rise
That all I do and all I say
Be pleasing to Thine eyes.
Amen.[6]

Dear Lord, I rise from bed to pray,
Then soon go out to school or play,

Let all I meet along the way,
See you in me throughout the day.[7]

Child's Prayer for Morning

Now, before I run to play,
Let me not forget to pray
To God who kept me through the night
And waked me with the morning light.
Help me, Lord, to love thee more
Than I ever loved before,
In my work and in my play
Be thou with me through the day.
Amen.

—Author Unknown[8]

Now I raise me up from sleep,
I thank the Lord who did me keep,
All through the night; and to Him pray
That He may keep me through the day.
All which for Jesus' sake, I say.
Amen.[9]

A Front-Door Blessing as Children Leave for School

The Lord bless you and
keep you from danger and sickness,

The Lord make His face shine in you,
and help you learn your lessons,

The Lord lift up His presence
in your life and give you happiness.
Amen.

Before Meals—Prayers of Thanksgiving for Children

Grant us Thy grace, O Lord, that, whether we eat or
drink, or whatsoever we do, we may do it all in Thy
name and to Thy glory.
Amen.[10]

O Bread of Life, from day to day
Be Thou our Comfort, Food, and Stay.
Amen.[11]

178

Child's Grace

God is great and God is Good,
And we thank God for our food;
By God's hand we must be fed,
Give us Lord, our daily bread.
Amen.

—Traditional[12]

Table Blessing

God is great! God is good!
Let us thank God for our food.
Amen.

—Traditional[13]

Keep Me Through the Day

Tender Jesus, meek and mild,
Look on me, a little child;
Help me, if it is Thy will,
To recover from all ill.
Amen.[14]

Keep my little tongue to-day,
Keep it gentle while I play;
Keep my hands from doing wrong.
Keep my feet the whole day long;
Keep me all, O Jesus mild,
Keep me ever Thy dear child.
Amen.[15]

Jesus, help my eyes to see
All the good Thou sendest me.
Jesus, help my ears to hear
Calls for help from far and near.
Jesus, help my feet to go
In the way that Thou wilt show.
Jesus, help my hands to do
All things loving, kind, and true.
Jesus, may I helpful be,
Growing every day like Thee.
Amen.[16]

Lamb of God, I look to Thee;
Thou shalt my example be;
Thou art gentle, meek, and mild,
Thou wast once a little child.

Fain I would be as Thou art:
Give me Thy obedient heart.
Thou art pitiful and kind:
Let me have Thy loving mind.

Loving Jesus, gentle Lamb,
In Thy gracious hands I am;
Make me, Savior, what Thou art,
Live Thyself within my heart.

I shall then show forth Thy praise,
Serve Thee all my happy days;
Then the world shall always see
Christ, the holy Child, in me.
Amen.[17]

Children's Bedtime Prayer

Now I lay me down to sleep,
I pray the Lord my soul to keep:
May God guard me through the night
And wake me with the morning light.
Amen.

—Traditional[18]

Bedtime Prayers

Now I lay me down to sleep;
I pray Thee, Lord, my soul to keep.
If I should die before I wake.
I pray Thee, Lord, my soul to take;
And this I ask for Jesus' sake.
Amen.[19]

All praise to Thee, my God, this night
For all the blessings of the light:
Keep me, O keep me, King of kings,
Beneath Thine own almighty wings.
Amen.[20]

At the End of the Day

At the close of every day,
Lord, to Thee I kneel and pray.
Look upon Thy little child,
Look in love and mercy mild.
O forgive and wash away
All my naughtiness this day,
And both when I sleep and wake
Bless me for my Savior's sake.
Amen.[21]

Be near me, Lord Jesus!
I ask Thee to stay
Close by me forever
And love me, I pray.
Bless all the dear children
In Thy tender care
And take us to heaven
To live with Thee there.
Amen.[22]

In my little bed I lie:
Heavenly Father, hear my cry;
Lord, keep Thou me through this night.
Bring me safe to morning light.
Amen.[23]

Salvation

Red is for the blood He gave,
Green is for the grass He made,
Yellow is for the sun so bright,
Orange is for the edge of night.

Black is for the sins that were made
White is for the grace He gave,
Purple is for the hour of sorrow,
Pink is for the new tomorrow.

Give a bag full of jelly beans,
Colorful and sweet,
Tell them it's a Prayer...
It's a promise...
It's an Easter Treat![24]

Endnotes

1. See http://www.prayer-and-prayers.info/prayers-for-children/be-near-me-lord-jesus.htm, (accessed 8 April 2009).

2. See http://www.feedyoursoul.org.uk/uploads/File/parenting.pdf, (accessed 20 April 2009).

3. Elmer Towns.

4. Elmer Towns.

5. See http://christianity.about.com/od/prayersforspecific needs/qt/morningprayers.htm, (accessed 14 April 2009).

6. See http://www.apples4theteacher.com/childrens-prayers/morning/, (accessed 14 April 2009).

7. See http://gidget.my100megs.com/cpr1.html, (accessed 14 April 2009).

8. See http://christianity.about.com/od/prayersforspecific needs/qt/morningprayers.htm, (accessed 14 April 2009).

9. See http://www.prayer-and-prayers.info/simple-short-prayers/now-i-raise-me-up-from-sleep.htm, (accessed 14 April 2009).

10. See http://www.apples4theteacher.com/childrens-prayers/table/before-meals/, (accessed 14 April 2009).

11. See http://www.apples4theteacher.com/childrens-prayers/table/before-meals/, (accessed 14 April 2009).

12. See http://www.godweb.org/prayersforchildren.htm, (accessed 14 April 2009).

13. See http://www.godweb.org/prayersforchildren.htm, (accessed 14 April 2009).

14. See http://www.prayer-and-prayers.info/prayers-for-children/tender-jesus-meek-and-mild.htm, (accessed 14 April 2009).

15. See http://www.prayer-and-prayers.info/prayers-for-children/keep-my-little-tongue-today.htm, (accessed 14 April 2009).

16. See http://www.prayer-and-prayers.info/simple-short-prayers/jesus-help-my-eyes-to-see.htm, (accessed 14 April 2009).

17. See http://www.prayer-and-prayers.info/prayers-for-children/lamb-of-god-i-look-to-thee.htm, (accessed 14 April 2009).

18. See http://www.godweb.org/prayersforchildren.htm, (accessed 14 April 2009).

19. See http://www.godweb.org/prayersforchildren.htm, (accessed 14 April 2009).

20. See http://www.prayer-and-prayers.info/prayers-for-children/at-the-close-of-every-day.htm, (accessed 14 April 2009).

21. See   http://www.prayer-and-prayers.info/prayers-for-children/at-the-close-of-every-day.htm, (accessed 14 April 2009).

22. See   http://www.prayer-and-prayers.info/prayers-for-children/be-near-me-lord-jesus.htm, (accessed 14 April 2009).

23. See   http://www.prayer-and-prayers.info/prayers-for-children/in-my-little-bed-i-lie.htm, (accessed 14 April 2009).

24. See   http://www.prayer-and-prayers.info/prayers-for-children/jelly-bean-prayer.htm, (accessed 14 April 2009).

I remember my mother's prayers and they have always followed me. They have clung to me all my life.

—Abraham Lincoln

(http://godweb.org/mothersdayprayer.htm)

Epilogue

One of the greatest praying couples for children was my (Elmer) father-in-law and mother-in-law, Elton and Elvira Forbes. He built houses for a living and she served Christ through Gideons International. But their greatest work for God was every morning after breakfast when they went into the living room and knelt by the sofa to pray for their children, and all their other prayer projects.

My wife, Ruth, remembers them praying for her when she was only five years old. They prayed for the man she would marry (me), that I'd be saved, and surrendered to do God's will. As Ruth grew older, they prayed her through junior high and senior high, and through college. They continued to pray for Ruth and

189

me after we were married, and into our child-raising years. I said on many occasions,

"Mr. and Mrs. Forbes are my greatest prayer support in ministry!"

They both died in 1981, and there were many things I missed about them, but the greatest was, "Who's going to be my prayer intercessor?"

God gave me a prayer team at my church, Thomas Road Baptist Church, Lynchburg, Virginia, and Buddy Bryant, a timberman, became my number one prayer partner.

Ruth and I became the prayer support team for our three children, then our ten grandchildren, and then for our three great grandchildren. The other day our youngest daughter Polly asked, "Who's going to pray for me when you die?"

Ruth answered her, "You'll have to pray for your family and your children, then your grandchildren." (Polly's children are both approaching their twenties, the age when children are born.)

We must do more than pray for our children, we must pass on our prayer heritage. They must learn to pray for themselves after their parents are gone, and then pray for their children's children.

The next generation can learn prayer from books, sermons, and Bible classes. They can learn it from CDs and tapes; but the greatest way for our children to learn how to pray for their children is from you as you daily talk to God about them.

When our children experience the results of prayer in their life, they will be motivated to pray for their children and grandchildren.

Let's all leave a legacy of prayer.

Top Ten Prayers

We did not put this list together but found it on the Web. We're not sure these are the top ten prayers. We might have included what the dishonest tax collector prayed in the Temple (the *King James Bible* called him the Publican). He wouldn't even lift his eyes toward Heaven, but prayed, "O God, be merciful to me a sinner."

We might have included the prayer that many have prayed, especially in children's ministry in our Western civilization, "Jesus come into my heart and save me."

Why Memorize Prayers?

Remember, children are eager to learn, there is a great passion in them to grow and become adults. While children are happy and mostly enjoy each and every moment, there is an insatiable appetite for growth. They learn, or memorize, things easier as children than they will ever do again in life. They will remember if you give a little effort to teach them.

And what better to learn than prayers that talk to God.

The finest prayer to teach children in this top ten list is the Lord's Prayer. Irenaeus (c. 115-c. 202) said we should teach children the Lord's Prayer when they begin to talk because it contains all the knowledge of God they need to know of Christianity, and it includes all the things they need to ask of God.

I (Elmer) have often said when preaching on the Lord's Prayer, "Just as the total oak tree is in the acorn, all of Christianity is in the Lord's Prayer."

[*Benediction: Thine is the Kingdom, power, and all the glory*]

The Lord's Prayer

Our Father, who art in heaven,

	1. Thy Name Hallowed	– worship
[*THY Section "In Heaven"*	2. Thy Kingdom Come	– guidance
	3. Thy Will be Done	– yield

Your name be hallowed
Your kingdom come,
Your will be done,
[*Semi-Conclusion: On Earth as it is in heaven.*]
on earth as it is in heaven.

[*Hinge:*	4. Give us daily bread	– provisions
	5. Forgive us	– pardon
{*US Section "On Earth"*	6. Lead us not	– victory
	7. Deliver us	– protection

Forgive us our debts, as we
forgive our debtors,
Lead us not into temptation,

192

Deliver us from the evil one,
[*Benediction: Thine is the Kingdom, power, and all the glory*]
for Yours is the kingdom
and the power and the glory, forever.
Amen.[1]

Matthew 6:9-13

Twenty-third Psalm

Lord be my shepherd, so I shall not want.

Make me lie down in green pastures;
Lead me beside still waters;
Restore my soul.

Lead me in right paths for Your name's sake.

Even when I walk through the valley
of the shadow of death,
I will fear no evil; for you are with me;
your rod and your staff comfort me.

You prepare a table before me
in the presence of my enemies;
you anoint my head with oil;
my cup overflows.

Surely Your goodness and mercy
shall follow me all the days of my life,

and I shall dwell in Your house
forever.[2]

Psalm 23:1-6

A Table Blessing

God is great and God is Good,
And we thank God for our food;
By God's hand we must be fed,
Give us Lord, our daily bread.
Amen.

—Traditional

A Short Grace for Use Before Meals

O Lord, bless this food to our use,
and us to your service;
make us grateful for all your mercies,
and mindful of the needs of others.
Amen.

—Anonymous

Bedtime Prayer

Now I lay me down to sleep,
I pray the Lord my soul to keep:
May God guard me through the night
and wake me with the morning light.
Amen.

—Traditional

Christ Be With Me

Christ with me, Christ before me, Christ behind me,
Christ in me, Christ beneath me, Christ above me,
Christ on my right, Christ on my left,
Christ where I lie, Christ where I sit, Christ where I arise,
Christ in the heart of everyone who thinks of me,
Christ in the mouth of everyone who speaks to me,
Christ in every eye that sees me,
Christ in every ear that hears me.

Salvation is of the Lord.

Salvation is of the Christ.

May your salvation, Lord, be ever with us.

—Saint Patrick

The Irish Blessing

May the road rise to meet you,
May the wind be always at your back,
May the sun shine warm upon your face,
The rains fall soft upon your fields and,
Until we meet again,
May God hold you in the palm of His hand.

—Anonymous

Make Me an Instrument of Your Peace

Lord, make me an instrument of your peace.

Where there is hatred, let me sow love,
Where there is injury, pardon,
Where there is doubt, faith,
Where there is despair, hope,
Where there is darkness, light,
Where there is sadness, joy,
O Divine Master, grant that I may not so much
seek to be consoled as to console,
not so much to be understood as to understand,
not so much to be loved, as to love;

196

for it is in giving that we receive,
it is in pardoning that we are pardoned,
it is in dying that we awake to eternal life.

—Saint Francis of Assisi

The Prayer of Jabez

Jabez called out to the God of Israel, "Oh that you
would bless me and enlarge my territory! Let your
hand be with me and keep me from harm, so that it
will not hurt me." And God granted what he asked.

1 Chronicles 4:10

The Jesus Prayer

Lord Jesus Christ, Son of God,
have mercy on me, a sinner.[3]

—This is one of the most universal prayers used
throughout Church history.

Endnotes

1. Elmer Towns, *Praying the Lord's Prayer for Spiritual Breakthrough* (Ventura, CA: Regal Books, 1997).

2. Elmer Towns, *Praying the 23rd Psalm* (Ventura, CA: Regal Books, 2001).

3. See http://www.godweb.org/toptenprayers.htm, (accessed 14 April 2009).

About Dr. Elmer Towns

Dr. Elmer Towns is an author of popular and scholarly works, a seminar lecturer, and dedicated worker in Sunday school. He has written over 130 books, including several best sellers, and he won the coveted Gold Medallion Book Award for *The Names of the Holy Spirit.*

Dr. Towns cofounded Liberty University with Jerry Falwell in 1971 and now serves as dean of the B.R. Lakin School of Religion and as distinguished professor of Theology and New Testament.

Liberty University was founded in 1971 and is the fastest-growing Christian university in America. Located in Lynchburg, Virginia, Liberty University is a private, coeducational, under-graduate and graduate institution offering 38 undergraduate and 15 graduate programs serving over 30,000 resident and external students (11,600 on campus). Individuals from all 50 states and more than 70 nations compose the diverse student body. While the faculty and students vary greatly, the common denominator and driving force of Liberty University since its conception is love for Jesus Christ and the desire to make Him known to the entire world.

For more information about Liberty University, contact:

Liberty University
1971 University Boulevard
Lynchburg, VA 24502
Telephone: 434-582-2000
Web site: www.Liberty.edu
e-mail: www.eltowns@liberty.edu.

About David Earley

David Earley is chairman of the Department of Pastoral Leadership at Liberty Baptist Theological Seminary and Liberty University. He also serves as the director of the Center for Church Planting of Liberty University. Previously, Dave served as the founding senior pastor of the New Life Church of Gahanna, Ohio. Dave has written 12 books, including *Prayer Odyssey* with Destiny Image.

Dave, and his wife, Cathy, have three highly active sons who are all studying ministry at Liberty University.

Additional copies of this book and other
book titles from DESTINY IMAGE are
available at your local bookstore.

Call toll-free: 1-800-722-6774.

Send a request for a catalog to:

Destiny Image® Publishers, Inc.

P.O. Box 310
Shippensburg, PA 17257-0310

*"Speaking to the Purposes of God for This
Generation and for the Generations to Come."*

**For a complete list of our titles,
visit us at www.destinyimage.com.**